IRELAND'S FRIENDLY DOLPHIN

You are helping dolphins when you buy this book. Half the author's royalties from this printing of Ireland's Friendly Dolphin go to the International Whale and Dolphin Conservation Society, a charity organization dedicated to making the world a safer place for our sea-going friends.

IRELAND'S Friendly DOLPHIN

Sean Mannion

BRANDON

The publishers wish to acknowledge the support of the ESB
in the publication of this book

First published in 1991 by
Brandon Book Publishers Ltd
Cooleen, Dingle, Co. Kerry

ISBN 0 86322 122 X

Cover designed by John Brady
Typeset by Seton Music Graphics, Bantry, Cork
Printed by Colour Books Ltd, Dublin

CONTENTS

OUT OF THE BLUE

IT WAS A clear, sunny autumn day. Off the west shore of *Tearaght*, an island ten miles out from the coast of Kerry in the far south-west of Ireland, the sea was sometimes brushed by a flurry of wind. Otherwise the day was calm.

A cormorant swam peacefully alone. Suddenly, a round, dark shape surfaced beside her, blocking out the sun. There was an explosive release of air and a jet of vapour shot skywards. Startled, the cormorant launched into a run across the water.

Behind her the dolphin watched the upset he had caused, but did not give chase; instead he lolled on the surface, letting the current carry him towards the island until he was about 200 metres off. Then, with an upward sweep of his tail, he resumed his journey. He passed between Inishnabro and the Great Blasket island. To the north was more land, to the east the expanse of Dingle Bay. He continued east.

Two miles further on the dolphin stopped again. He scanned the sea ahead with his sonar. Answering echoes alerted him. His head twitched quickly from right to left, his brain absorbing the returning data. He emitted a series of measured sounds, notes of pure tone spaced at one-second intervals. There was a large object almost out of range moving to the north. With a great beat of his tail he headed for it.

He travelled fast – 25 knots – leaping out of the water to take in air without losing speed or direction. The echoes coming from the target were now more defined. It was still heading north, at about five knots. Soon the dolphin could see it. It was shaped a little like a bowl and was ploughing through the surface, leaving a wide trail of wash behind. A fishing trawler.

The dolphin darted up to the bow of the boat and began to ride its wave, dipping his tail down for a free push through the water. After a short while he let himself drop back behind the vessel before stroking powerfully up to the large, spinning propeller blades. He studied their shape and motion intently, directing bursts of high-pitched sound to each one in turn.

Above in the trawler's wheelhouse the crewmen were puzzled by the outbreak of activity on their sonar screen. Moments later the dolphin's sickle-shaped dorsal fin was spotted from the deck. A young man, bucket in hand, was standing at the stern, his finger pointing at the dolphin. An older man came out of the wheelhouse, shading his eyes from the sun. They watched the dolphin jump alongside the boat, almost touching it as he danced with the wash. The older man bent down to pick up something. He threw it towards the dolphin.

The dolphin diverted from the ship to investigate. It was a dead pollock. He examined it for a while but he had no interest in a lifeless meal. His main interest, the fishing boat, had ploughed on. The dolphin forged ahead in pursuit.

Land was beginning to close in on both sides; they were entering a harbour. Sensing the shallowness, the dolphin broke away and swam back to the harbour's mouth. Just outside and to the east was a small bay area which he began to explore. Suddenly he took a deep, vertical dive, turned and raced back up. He speared through the surface and flew high into the new atmosphere, the sun flashing on the films of water coating his body as he climbed to the highest point. He hung at the summit a split second longer than seemed possible; then, swinging his body around, he began a head-first downward plunge, re-entering the water with little disturbance. He jumped four times before resting.

He detected a shoal of fish nearby. He was about to give chase when another sound distracted him. It was the newly familiar, loud chugging noise he had heard half an hour before. This time a fishing trawler was leaving the harbour. The dolphin set off after it.

FISHERMEN'S FRIEND

FEW DOLPHINS EVER venture into Dingle harbour. Over the years small herds of Bottlenose and Common dolphins had been seen approaching the harbour's mouth, but there they checked and turned back out as if suddenly sensing the shallowness of the water and the nearness of the land. The Harbour porpoise, a smaller cousin of the dolphin, proved an exception to this rule. Herds of these *tóithín* – as they are called locally – were seen doing "a lap" of the harbour in the 1960s, racing and leaping into its far reaches in pursuit of fish.

Dolphins are seen more frequently outside the harbour, in Dingle Bay, and the boats that fish out of the ports on the south and west coasts of the bay have had regular contact with various species. The most frequent encounters have been with Common and Bottlenose dolphins. Herds of the black-and-white-coloured Common dolphin, each numbering between one and two hundred, were spotted in the Blasket Sound in September 1990, as indeed was a lone Fin whale, locally referred to as a "herring hog". During the late '70s one Bottlenose dolphin had stayed at the mouth of Dingle harbour for a few days, but it disappeared out to sea again. Then, a few years later, during the winter of 1983, the fishermen noticed something unusual happening at the entrance to the harbour.

The Dingle fishermen form a special, closely knit community whose centre lies not in the town itself but among all the fishing ports of the south-west coast. They are a tough breed of men, hardened by their experiences at sea. On shore they are a spirited bunch intent on enjoying life, all the more so because they know just how perilous life can be.

They harvest the sea according to the seasons. White fish – cod, whiting, hake and megrims –

are fished from March to June; from then until September the fishermen turn to shellfish – lobster, crab and crawfish. Through the autumn and winter months, from September to February, the boats trawl mackerel and herring. The income from the catch is shared out among the crew; this tradition is still maintained, unlike the practice of paying a wage or percentage which is the norm today in Dublin or in Spanish ports.

The fishing tradition is long-established: hake and salmon from Dingle were presented as gifts to the King of Spain in the 17th century. It is a tradition that runs deep in the town and influences all the villages and townlands of the peninsula. At Christmas-time salted ling or pollock is served as a reminder of the days when a goose could not be afforded as a Christmas meal. The fishing community welcomes the sea's bounty and respects the sea's power: a bottle of holy water is carried by every boat of the fleet.

The fishermen come across many strange creatures on their sea-bound travels. Thus they did not pay much attention when, towards the end of 1983, they began to see a fin in the water around the boats. Some remarked that they had seen a shark following them, but this was not unusual: a shark's powerful sense of smell would draw him to the scent of blood from the catch on board. The fishermen were too busy filleting fish or throwing away waste catch to watch the prowler in earnest.

In December the German market for herring collapsed and the trawlers' catches remained unsold at the pier. They had to be dumped back into the sea before they began to rot. The boats took their unwanted catches outside the harbour's mouth and began off-loading. As they did so, sudden bursts of activity appeared on their sonar screens. Some object among the sinking fish was generating sound. At that depth it could hardly have been a submarine. The fishermen were puzzled by this unexplained interference.

12/   The mystery soon resolved itself. A fisherman looking over the side of his boat saw a dark

shadow rising through the water. It broke the surface and emitted a loud blow of air. It was a dolphin.

The lone mammal had been in the area when it discovered its environment being suddenly deluged with fish. Excited, it raced around and among the shoals, firing sound-beams at each sinking mass, and this had caused the activity on the boat's sonar. The dolphin didn't appear to eat any of the dead fish but several times he caught one in his mouth, surfaced and flung it into the air. One or two fish even landed back on the decks of the craft that had dumped them.

Spotting the dolphin jogged some fishermen's memories: *this* was the creature that had been following the boats. They laughed and clapped at the dolphin's antics, and when they turned back for port he followed them part of the way.

Over the next few days crews on board each boat reported having the dolphin for company as they set out fishing. He would escort them out as far as the Crow Rock, a cluster of rock jutting above the surface two miles west of the harbour's mouth. There the dolphin would break off and head back. When the boats returned they found the dolphin waiting for them at the same rock and he would accompany them to the mouth of the harbour before again breaking off.

"He'd start jumping high in the air way ahead of you as you came in," one fisherman remembers. "Then he would swim fast towards you. About 30 yards ahead he would stop in the water, waiting for you to come along. When we came up with him he would start swimming just ahead or alongside. We got used to meeting him. If he didn't come out we'd miss his welcome."

Soon the sprightly dolphin was leaping and playing around all the fishing boats. It was inquisitive as well as being playful. Skipper Patrick Sheehy was out crab fishing on board the *Roving Swan*.

"We were cutting the crabs' claws before putting them into a storage tank," he recalls.

"Suddenly the dolphin leapt into the air right beside us. It was as if he was trying to get a look at what we were doing."

On other occasions, when the boat's engines were stopped, Patrick and his crew mates would be puzzled by a tapping noise coming from the stern. "The propellers were turning slowly because of the flowing tide. We'd look down and there would be the dolphin, hitting each turning blade with his beak. As soon as the tide turned and the propellers stopped moving he disappeared."

A robust and exuberant flying dolphin had entered the lives of the fishermen, who now encountered him more and more. "We were going out around dawn on board the *Seafisher*," recalls Paddy Garvey. "I was on the deck looking out to sea with my cap on and a cigarette in my mouth. It was the most peaceful, quiet morning you could imagine. Suddenly the dolphin rushed straight out of the water right under my nose." Paddy's cap and cigarette were sent flying.

Martin Flannery had a similar dawn experience while going out salmon fishing with his son Bruce on board their boat, the *Taimh Rialtóir*. "We had just got down to the harbour's mouth when we saw the dolphin," says Martin. "He was jumping crazy." As the boat was heading out of the harbour Martin stuck his head out of the wheelhouse window to see if he could spy the dolphin. He got more than he bargained for. "The dolphin just shot up below my head. He knocked the pipe out my mouth with his belly."

There were other close encounters. Fisherman Donie Flaherty was steering the *Anne Patricia* when he looked over the side and almost connected with an uppercut as the dolphin launched himself out of the water. Sometimes Fungie's carefree behaviour could be too much. One fisherman says wryly: "On Monday mornings the fishermen sailing out might not be in the best of moods after having a few drinks and a few late nights over the weekend. The dolphin would often shoot up and give them the shock of their lives, and then he'd start jumping all

over the place full of the joys of spring! A lot of bad language went after him on those mornings."

The *Maicréal*, a white 26-foot launch owned by Paudie Curran and his son Packie, got special attention from the newcomer. The Currans were out hauling lobster pots at eight o'clock one summer's morning when, with the ease of a showjumper clearing a fence, the dolphin leapt over the middle of their boat. At that point the boat was three feet high and eight feet across. Neither of the men saw the jump – Paudie was bending down and Packie had his back turned – but Patrick Sheehy on board the passing *Roving Swan* did.

Father and son did see it when the dolphin jumped a second time a couple of months later. "My father was steering the boat and I was at the bow," Packie recalls. "All of a sudden the dolphin leapt into the air and over the boat. Our hearts nearly stopped. We felt like keeping our heads down after that." The jump was also seen by Laurence Courtney on board the *Naomh Deracha*. And years later, in August 1990, the dolphin cleared the stern of the boat, much to the shock of Mary, a relative of Paudie and Packie who was on a trip home from America and who was standing close to the point over which the dolphin jumped.

Although he sometimes gave them surprises that made their hearts skip a beat, the fishermen enjoyed the dolphin's company from the start. "He was a character," says Patrick Sheehy. "You couldn't come in or out of the harbour without seeing the dolphin's head as high as the level of the wheelhouse window, as if he was trying to look in at you."

News of the dolphin's escapades at sea soon became such a talking point in the town that one day a visitor asked if it had a name. Not wishing to disappoint the enquirer, a Dingle citizen thought one up. "Fungie," he said. It was, in fact, a fisherman's nickname, given to him on account of his beard. No one at the time ever dreamt that the name would stick, nor indeed become famous. But Fungie it was and Fungie it has remained.

SHARK!

To the east of Dingle town lies *Binn Bán* strand, a small, sandy beach tucked between the cliffs of rocky headlands. The favourite bathing place of people from the town, it was crowded one summer's day with about 60 people who had taken advantage of the warm weather.

Rosemary O'Keeffe was one of those who went in for a swim, making her way out from the shore through the gentle waves that rolled in and sent occasional bursts of spray flying up from the rocks to the left and right. The cove was filled with summer sounds: the waves rippling on the shore, voices calling and laughing in the water, the squealing of children on the beach and seagulls calling as they flew around the cliffs.

Rosemary was only in the water a few minutes when she sensed that something was wrong. She did not recognize what it was for a moment, but then it struck her: the voices. They were still coming from the shore but they were different – they were calling in urgent shouts. She looked back. All the people on the beach had gathered at the shore. They were calling out and pointing over Rosemary's head. She turned again and looked out to sea, thinking that a swimmer might be in difficulty. There was nobody in the sea further out. She scanned the area.

She had not spotted it at first, merging with the waves, but now she saw it clearly. Its curved, blade-like shape cut through the water – a shark fin.

One word struck Rosemary's mind: *Jaws*!

"I had been in the water before when porpoises would come in close. I could see the back as well as the fin on this thing. It was huge, much bigger than a porpoise."

/19

Anxious though not panicking, Rosemary swam quickly back to shore. The other swimmers did so too, swimming, splashing and wading hurriedly to the safety of land. From there the crowd watched the finned back rolling over the water, neither coming near nor drawing away as it patrolled the shore.

A few days later the swimmers were back at *Binn Bán*. Again the fin appeared, following the same route it had taken before. "Everyone got out again, except for a few men who were braver this time and stayed a little longer," says Rosemary.

Jimmy Flannery was just as quick as anyone else to get out of the water when the dolphin approached. "People nowadays don't realize how frightened everybody was of this creature swimming not far from you. No one took any chances – you got out of the water quickly!"

Across from *Binn Bán* lies the point of the headland which is known as the Toureen Bán, a favourite spot for anglers. But one rod fisherman got a fright when, reeling in his line, he saw the bait being pursued by a large fin! Early encounters like these almost proved to be the dolphin's undoing. One Dingle man became convinced that the creature was a threat to safety and he decided to do something about it. It was only by chance that he happened to meet one of the fishermen before putting his plan into action.

"He told me," recalls the fisherman, "that there was a Blue shark in the area and that he was going to take his shotgun out in the morning and do away with him."

The fisherman appealed to the man not to shoot the creature. "I told him it was a dolphin that had been friendly with the fishing boats. He was only going near swimmers because he was curious." The man was finally persuaded to leave his shotgun at home. Another person, annoyed that the paint was being worn away from the bow of his boat by Fungie constantly rubbing off it, was also dissuaded from taking drastic action.

20/ As the swimmers and others became more aware of the dolphin's harmlessness the retreat from the beaches at *Sláidín* and *Binn Bán* was reversed. "Before the dolphin came there would be no more than 20 people at *Sláidín*," recalls Jimmy Flannery, "and when he appeared there would be nobody there because of him. Now, because of him, there are hundreds."

THE LIGHTHOUSEKEEPER

FUNGIE'S FIRST TWO years in Dingle harbour passed quietly and he spent much of his time exploring his new home, visiting every crag and inlet on the coastline of his territory.

The entrance to the harbour is marked by a lighthouse on the east side; on the Burnham headland to the west stands Eask Tower, a tower of solid stone with a wooden hand projecting from it and pointing out the dangerous, "blind" harbour's mouth. The dolphin adopted one of the coves east of the lighthouse, Gravelly Cuas, as his base and patrolled it constantly during the first few months of his stay. He only broke from these patrols when a fishing boat passed by or when, as the summer came, swimmers began to gather further east at *Binn Bán*.

Gradually he began to move out further and explore, crossing the harbour's mouth to the Burnham shore. He did not venture far into the harbour because of the water's shallowness, but he roamed to the west, investigating the rugged rocks and cliffs which drop into Dingle Bay. A sea-stack at Burnham, the Toureen Bán, marks the boundary of harbour and open sea; from here the rocky banks of the harbour rise steeply to commanding precipices, great slabs of soaring sandstone that overlook the panorama of the bay. Away to the south the mountains of the Iveragh peninsula draw a trail of sweeping curves on the horizon.

These places around Fungie's new home had Gaelic names, many of them revealing miniature histories of past generations' lives. Like *An Dochtúir* (The Doctor), a cliff called after a highly respected but non-qualified medical man of the last century. Or *Pointe an Allais* (the Sweating Point), the point at which fishermen rowing out the harbour had to strain hard against the headwind coming in off the bay.

Travelling west from the Toureen Bán the dolphin would circle *An Tiompán* (the Drum), whose broad back gave rowers shelter and respite from the wind. The sickle-shaped fin marked his progress as he swam around the ledges and outcrops of rock. He might idle at the Tailor's Table, a flat layer of rock on which was mounted a triangular-shaped stone known as the Iron, then progress to the Blowhole, where water sweeping over a hole in the rock was shot back out as if from a cannon.

The dolphin would pass beyond *Carraig Tuite* (Tuite's Rock) and *Pointe Mháire* (Mary's Point) and then, at the furthest point of his travels, disappear through a narrow entrance into *Cuas Fothrom na Tóirní*. Fungie spent long periods inside this impressive cove; cut into the cliffs, the enclosed space amplified the sound of the waves drumming against its walls. The old generation's name for it was apt: The Cove of the Thunderous Waves.

By the second year of his stay Fungie had established the harbour's mouth as his constant base, and from here he explored not only the coastline but also anything that drifted into his area of sea. He would nose a stray frond of seaweed for hours, pushing it against the tide, leaving it and then following after it. When he came across a patch of foam he would break it up by diving several times into its middle.

Often, if the tide was flowing out, he would go up to the Black Point, an outstretch of rock in the harbour channel. There the fast-flowing waters rounding the point were broken into waves on the lower side and Fungie would catch onto a wave and let it carry him down. As soon as the wave rode out near the point below the lighthouse he would swim back up again to catch another. If the sea was more turbulent he would often go out to *Binn Bán* and be carried close to shore by stronger waves. Sometimes he would hang vertical in the water, his head above the surface, while passing waves raised and lowered him. Even on calm days he would "spy-hop" off Binn Bán strand, sticking his head above the water and looking towards the house-dotted landscape for long periods.

The incoming tide brought fish with it, and Fungie became the hunter then. His back rolled fleetingly on the surface every half-minute as he dived in pursuit of prey. He would catch each fish from behind, puncturing its flesh with his teeth, then – to avoid its spiny fins catching in his throat – he would twist it around before swallowing it whole.

His hunger satisfied, Fungie would still catch another fish, and this one would become his personal plaything. He would hold onto it for anything up to half an hour, first letting it sink and then diving to retrieve it. Sometimes he would toss the fish into the air, either catching it in his mouth as it came down or letting it drop beside him.

With a bigger fish Fungie might act as if he was involved in a heroic struggle. He would emerge suddenly from the water with a wriggling strip of silver flashing in his mouth, throw it forward with a jerk of his head and chase after it. Prey and hunter would seem to twist, turn and thrash around in the water before disappearing below, the foaming patch of water on top marking the continuing battle underneath.

On days when the water was calm Fungie would "lobtail", raising his tail high into the air and bringing it down flat against the surface with a deep, loud smack that sent spray flying high into the air. His head would remain underwater to detect any fish the noise might have disturbed from cover.

He might start jumping at any time, night or day. A bright calm sunny morning, however, seemed to provide the ideal conditions for a jumping spree. The jumps could range from one huge leap out of the water, reaching up to twelve feet in height, to a series of between three and ten smaller jumps. Often he would spend a whole morning jumping, taking short periods of rest. Calm evenings were Fungie's next most favoured time, though a fishing boat approaching might also spur him into action at any hour of the day.

Sometimes Fungie would lie listless on calm waters for long periods, his body either on its

side or the upper half lurking above the water like a submarine. Even the boats would not stir him then. If he sensed people on the shore he would often move in to where the depth was no more than three feet and the land just four or five yards away. There he would adopt the submarine posture, the upper half of his body above the water-line and facing land all the time. To the people on the beach this looked both sinister and humorous.

No one has observed Fungie in all his moods more than Paddy Ferriter, the Dingle lighthouseman, whose lighthouse stands above the harbour's mouth and offers a grandstand view of Fungie's home. Paddy has an intimate, daily knowledge of a species of wild creature which is seldom seen so close to land for so long.

Now in his 70s Paddy was once a fisherman himself, going out in a rowing boat with his father to haul lobster pots. Although age has curbed his travels, in his mind he can walk from *Sláidín* through *Binn Bán* to Minard, some eight miles to the east, naming and relating the lore of every tiny inlet, rock or headland on the way in the manner of a gifted storyteller.

Paddy remembers when he first saw the dolphin. "About noon one day I happened to be at the wall outside the lighthouse. I heard a blowing sound, looked around and saw a dolphin in the water just below the lighthouse. I took no special notice of him, I'd seen dolphins before. I went in, had tea and came out again. He was still there. I remember saying to him, 'you look like a bloke that's going to put down your moorings here for the night'."

Paddy was surprised to see him remain there all the next day. Yet in the years that have followed he has seen him almost every single day, and during wet and stormy weather the dolphin has often been Paddy's only company.

"Those first two years nobody paid much attention to him. He would go by the boats up and down each day. If he went near any of the swimmers at *Sláidín* they would all get out of the water very quickly I can tell you."

Paddy Ferriter

The old lighthouseman watched the dolphin satisfy his curiosity about humans, other sea creatures and alien objects which passed through his adopted home ground. A lobster fisherman couldn't haul his pots without Fungie nosing around them like a sniffer dog. Everything from a piece of plastic to a thousand-ton Naval Service ship was subjected to his thorough examination. Paddy was especially impressed by one particular feat of strength.

"There was a good stiff sou'-west wind blowing one afternoon and a strong tide was going up. Nobody was in the harbour. I was watching a fine big log, about eight or nine feet, going with the tide. I knew it would draw into *Sláidín* and I could go down and get it for the fire. But then the dolphin appeared beside it. He made a few leaps over it and examined it. Then he stood back from it and ran into it, hitting it in the middle with his beak. He hit it again and again, driving it down against the tide. The waves didn't bother him in the slightest.

"He got the log to the mouth of the harbour. I was annoyed with him because once the log would pass the point it would drift over to *Binn Bán* and others would be able to pick it up for firewood. 'Blast you anyway!' I called out to him. 'Why don't you leave the log alone?' But once he did reach the mouth he seemed to lose interest. I managed to get it in the end where it drifted up at Gravelly Cuas."

Paddy has often seen the dolphin playing with cormorants. "I remember one poor cormorant trying to swim ashore and Fungie pushing it down time after time. The cormorant made it to shore but that finished them as far as I was concerned. I thought Fungie had malice for them. Then one day I saw something on the lad's back. I got out my spy-glass and saw it was a cormorant. Its wings were spread for balance as Fungie moved slowly forward. Then the dolphin just turned on its side and the cormorant slipped into the water. Another time, too, I saw about a dozen cormorants swimming together – it would be rare to see that happening. The

next thing the dolphin came along. The cormorants separated for him and Fungie passed through like a king. They closed up again afterwards."

On a calm night the sounds of a dolphin blowing for air or leaping and splashing in the water travel down the chimney and out through the range in Paddy's lighthouse. "I would often go out to see if I could see him. It might be too dark but if there was a moon I would see the white splashes where he was jumping, like fire in the water."

Some people in Dingle believe that Fungie remained because he lost his partner in the area. If that is so Paddy might be one of very few people to have seen it. One day in late September 1983 he walked down to a cove on the *Binn Bán* side of the lighthouse. "There is a well on top where I can draw fresh water," he says. On this trip he spotted a dolphin washed up on the gravel below. He went down to it. "It was a huge dolphin, as big as Fungie," he says. "Its head was facing out to sea." Paddy put his hand on its side. The skin was still fresh, so it hadn't been dead for long. "There wasn't a scratch on it although I couldn't see the other side."

Paddy wasn't too bothered about the discovery. He had come across other dolphins washed ashore before. "I often worry what would I do if I found a large dolphin alive. I found two young dead dolphins once. If they had been alive I could have carried them back to the sea. With a big dolphin like that one I found below the well you'd need two strong men to put it back in."

Paddy drew water from the well and went home. The following days were wet and the rain-barrels supplied his water needs. When he did go back a few days later the body was gone, the sea probably having reclaimed its own.

Paddy often wonders what would happen if other live dolphins came into the area. Would Fungie go with them or would he stay? "Several times I've seen dolphins swim in here before, but not since 'your man' came. Who knows, instead of him leaving the other dolphins might stay. What would we do with a couple of friendly dolphins?"

MAKING FRIENDS

As Fungie's presence became more and more a part of the place, swimmers overcame their fear and tried to swim with him at *Binn Bán*. But, like a rainbow, the dolphin was always moving out of reach. Soon, however, four sub aqua divers began to take an interest: Brian Holmes and Sheila Stokes, and Ronnie Fitzgibbon and John O'Connor.

Originally from England, Brian Holmes and Sheila Stokes had been attracted by the unspoilt Irish seaboard and had come to live in Cork. Their first encounter with dolphins came when, as Brian was carrying out a survey on the Shannon estuary, two of them leapt out of the water beside him. He contacted Sheila who came down that weekend to swim with the dolphins.

Dolphin fever had gripped them. The following summer they travelled to Clifden to follow up reports of a herd of dolphins seen around Ballinakill Bay. They saw fins on the horizon on the first day and then nothing more. On the last-but-one day of the trip they heard of "porpoises" being sighted at Little Killary harbour. They packed their gear into the van and took off. As they drove down a narrow, looping road towards a coral strand they saw the finned, arched backs of dolphins rolling on the surface in the bay.

They changed into their wetsuits and swam out. The dolphins shied away from them, disappearing into the darkness of the sea. After trying fruitlessly to find the wild creatures the couple returned to the shore and changed out of their wetsuits. Just then they spotted the dolphins again jumping out in the bay. Back into the water they went, but out at sea the dolphins repeated their disappearing act.

Brian Holmes and Sheila Stokes

"We decided to float around for ten minutes before swimming back," says Brian. "Suddenly the water just erupted with 20 faces. They shot by us like bullets in the water. I remember shouting, 'Oh my God!' I was nervous and had to keep reminding myself that nobody had ever been deliberately hurt by a dolphin."

The experience lasted an hour and quickly turned from fright to thrill. In the days that followed they spent every moment they could in the water with the dolphins. Reluctant ever to leave the creatures that had given them so much joy, they overstayed their holiday by three days.

They returned the next summer, 1986, but the herd had vanished. "We made it a policy thereafter of asking people anywhere we'd go to if there were dolphins in the area," says Sheila. By chance they went to Dingle, where the fishermen told them of a lone dolphin living out in the harbour.

It was the beginning of a long acquaintance. The dolphin was shy but curious at the initial overtures from two humans in the water, steering around the wetsuit-clad couple but keeping out of reach. As the trips mounted and the rapport progressed Fungie overcame his natural caution and allowed himself to be touched. Those were happy days for the couple when a swim into the middle of the harbour's mouth would draw a visit from this creature of the wild. Later, as Fungie's fame drew more and more swimmers and divers to Dingle, their time alone with the dolphin began to shorten, and their time alone became all the more precious for that.

John O'Connor, a local ESB electrician with a love of diving, had also heard the stories about the dolphin from the fishermen. Like almost everyone else in Dingle he did not give the stories much thought until one day he was out swimming with his daughter, Deirdre. "We had swum out towards *Binn Bán* Head where we rested on some rocks for a while. Then when we started to swim back for shore this beautiful dolphin swam under Deirdre. It turned on its back underwater and looked up at her."

John O'Connor (in yellow mac) introduces the dolphin

Both were captivated by the experience. John contacted his diving friend, Ronnie Fitzgibbon, who lived in Tralee, 30 miles away. Ronnie was a national snorkelling officer with the Irish Underwater Council and had over 25 years diving experience. The two friends decided to swim with the dolphin as much as they could.

The fruits of that experience are recounted in Ronnie's book, *The Dingle Dolphin*, a personal account of getting to know a wild but gentle creature. John pays Ronnie tribute for doing most of the work. "I lived locally," he says, "but Ronnie would travel out from Tralee, day after day for two years in hail, rain or snow to try and befriend Fungie."

By the summer of 1986 the dolphin was beginning to be well known in Dingle. Many had seen him as they took the favourite Dingle walk from the town out along the shore of the harbour to *Sláidín*. On 26 July of that year an event took place which gave many people their first close-up view of Fungie. A festival called *Dúchas an Daingin* was held to celebrate the town's history and culture, and as part of it the tradition of the "Blessing of the Boats" was revived.

Dingle's link with the sea has always been important. For centuries the harvest from the bay has provided livelihoods for many of the townspeople. The fishermen put aside one day of the year, usually the Sunday closest to the feast of St Peter the Fisherman on 29 June, to give thanks and show respect to their provider. The tradition had lapsed in recent years, but now the ceremony had returned to the town.

Dingle was decorated with banners and streamers as marching bands made up of boys and girls from Dingle and Lispole paraded along the narrow streets winding down to the pier. Here the parish priest blessed the boats that made up the fishing fleet. Then the boats took on board as many of the townspeople as wished to go out on a trip to the harbour's mouth.

The boats themselves were as colourful and decorative as the streets, each bedecked in bunting. Some carried the girls and boys of the marching bands and other musicians, and the sound of their playing carried across the waves. Once the fleet reached the bay it formed a circle around the boat which carried the priest. He began to bless the bay, uttering a prayer in Latin blessing the sea, its creatures, and the harvest. As he solemnly intoned this prayer, a murmur of wonder rose up among the crowd.

A dolphin had emerged from the water and was swimming and leaping all round the boats. It was as if the sea had sent one of its own, the sacred messenger of the ancient world, to attend the ceremony. Many who had not seen the dolphin, or indeed any dolphin before at close quarters, watched in awe. From that day on there were very few who did not know that a distinguished visitor was in their midst.

LEGEND AND LORE

IN ANCIENT TIMES the dolphin was highly honoured and respected. The civilizations of the Minoans from Crete and the Mycenaeans of mainland Greece flourished between 5,000 and 3,000 years ago. Both seafaring peoples, their most important objects were very often decorated with dolphins. Shields, cups, vases and coins all bore the dolphin's image and in the palace of Knossos on the island of Crete the beautiful fresco in the queen's room was decorated with dolphins.

The dolphin was important to them in many ways. In Greece the deliberate killing of a dolphin was treated the same as the killing of a human, and in many Greek legends the gods, particularly Apollo, took on the form of dolphins. The Cretans named the oracle which they regarded as the centre of the universe Delphi – the place of the dolphin.

In life and in death the dolphin was a welcome figure. The word dolphin is related to the classical Greek word *delphis*, meaning womb, the beginning of life. And it seems, too, the dolphin was believed to deliver the human soul to paradise after death. The presence of a dolphin at a ship's prow was a good omen for a voyage, and dolphins were known to have led back to safety ships which had been lost at sea.

The Phoenician and Greek civilizations that followed also regarded the dolphin with great respect. Dozens of Greek towns featured the dolphin on their coins. One coin from ancient Syracuse (480–400 BC) shows the head of the goddess Arethusa surrounded by four dolphins. A Greek cup which was crafted in about 500 BC depicts the legend of the god Dionysus who, when at sea, realized that his crew planned to sell him into slavery. He turned their oars into

/39

serpents and, terrified, the sailors jumped into the sea where they were rescued by Poseidon, the god of the sea, who turned them into dolphins. Full of remorse for plotting against Dionysus and grateful to Poseidon, they promised to become friendly to human beings.

Aristotle, one of the greatest of the classical writers, studied dolphins, and it was he who first realized that they and whales were mammals, not fish. He also distinguished between dolphins and porpoises. One of the stories he told was about a dolphin which was caught by fishermen and brought into harbour. A herd of dolphins followed the boat and would not leave until their captured friend was freed. Moved by the display, the fishermen released the dolphin.

The Romans borrowed from the Greek legends and they, too, honoured the dolphin in their pottery and coins. Tales of the dolphin's good-will, intelligence and friendliness abound in stories from Homer to Herodotus and *Aesop's Fables*. The Roman naturalist, Pliny the Elder, was the first to provide a documentary account of the behaviour of dolphins. In his 37-volume book, *Naturalis Historia*, he told the story of a boy from a town near Naples who was in the habit of going to Lake Lucrino to feed a dolphin called Simo, who would give him a ride on his back to school on the other side of the lake. One day the boy did not come: he had died from sickness during the night. As the days passed and the boy still did not appear the dolphin mourned him deeply and eventually died from grief at the loss of his friend.

In Homer's tale of Ulysses, the hero's son, Telemachus, falls into the sea and is rescued by a dolphin. In gratitude Ulysses always wore a ring afterwards with a dolphin engraved on it. In another story Pliny's adopted son, Pliny the Younger, tells a friend in a letter about a young boy who had been saved from drowning at Hippo, a seaport in Tunisia. The dolphin and the boy became friends and the townsfolk would congregate on the beaches to watch the lively pair dive and swim together, and some would wade into the sea to pet the dolphin.

The most powerful and moving story of a dolphin's love for a child was the story of "The Dolphin Rider". In Iassos, a town on the south-west coast of present-day Turkey but which was then part of Greece, a school lay near a beach. After school and play the children used to wash and bathe in the sea before they went home. One week a dolphin started to appear close to the children in the water and to follow one boy in particular. This boy was afraid and would run out of the water when it approached. But soon he overcame his fears and they quickly became friends. The boy would swim with the dolphin, get on his back and be taken far out to sea. Then the dolphin would carry the boy back, leave him on the shore and return to the open sea.

Every day when school was over the dolphin waited for his friend. The whole town of Iassos admired the dolphin and boy at play together. But then one day, excited and tired, the boy fell on his friend's dorsal fin and it pierced his stomach. The dolphin felt the boy heavy on him and saw the blood in the water. He swam quickly towards shore and threw himself and the boy up on the beach in an effort to save him, and there they were found together, the boy dead and the dolphin dying. The people of Iassos built a tomb for the two friends and mounted on it a stone engraved with a picture of them. Later they minted coins to commemorate them.

Stories of girls and dolphins do not feature much in historic tales but they do in modern life. In 1945 at Long Island South in the United States a 13-year-old girl, Sally Stone, made friends with a dolphin. Ten years later in Hokianga Bay, New Zealand, another 13-year-old, Jill Baker, was the favourite friend of Opo, a dolphin who used to dive under her and give her rides through the water.

The most famous wild dolphin of all was called Pelorus Jack, and he was of a variety called a Risso's dolphin. Though he never actually swam near humans, from 1888 this dolphin guided ships through Cook Strait in New Zealand for all of 25 years. He was mentioned in articles by writers Rudyard Kipling and Mark Twain, and he became famous all over the world.

"Flipper", a Bottlenose dolphin whose adventures were featured in an American TV series first shown over 20 years ago, is perhaps the greatest dolphin "legend" of all. Like most legends, Flipper never really existed – he was played by several different dolphins – but it was he alone who raised human interest in dolphins to levels it had only enjoyed some 2,000 years before in ancient Greece.

Yet dolphins do still make their homes close to coastal towns and villages and they do still befriend humans. But for all the long history of contact between the two, getting the opportunity to meet a wild dolphin is a chance in a lifetime.

UNDERWATER WORLD

AFTER SEEING FUNGIE several times from a boat, I decided finally to try to meet him in his own world. I climbed down the ladder at Dingle pier and hopped on board the dolphin boat. There were four other passengers – a girl from Hamburg, an English couple and an Irishman. The boat's engine started up, the ropes were untied and we steered gently past the moored fishing boats and out into the harbour.

The boat rose and fell gently over the waves. The clear cold morning sharpened our senses. As we moved further out the buildings on the shore began to merge into a town, then the town itself merged into the landscape. The mountains rose up behind, each joined to the other by meandering ridges. By this time we had reached the end of our outward trail. As the boat slowed we turned our attention away from the mountains and down towards the harbour's mouth. The engine had quietened down to a low drone and the passengers' happy conversations had died away. There was now a thin air of suspense on board; we were floating over the dolphin's world.

The English couple scanned the sea on one side of the boat; the Irish and German trio watched on the other. He could come from any direction. His arrival might be signalled from a distance by his blade-like dorsal fin, or he might erupt in a sudden, explosive leap right beside our boat. Everyone on the boat was alert, even tense.

The dolphin did not appear.

We waited for 15 minutes and then Martin, the boatman, decided that the dolphin must be out in the bay. The engine came to life and we headed out into the open sea. The stiffer waves outside began to push the boat around. Looking at them I began to have second and even third

thoughts about having said that I would get into a wetsuit; I didn't like the idea of swimming in water as rough and deep as this.

There was still no sign of Fungie. Martin called an incoming trawler on the radio. No, they hadn't seen the dolphin either. We were about to turn and head back to the harbour when a cry went up: "There he is!"

We followed the pointed finger eagerly. There, cutting its way elegantly through the waves on our starboard side, was the slate-grey, finned back of the dolphin. He was coming quickly towards the boat like someone who was late for an appointment. Everyone cheered at once.

We couldn't see much of him in the rough seas of the bay, so Martin decided to try to get him to follow us back into the harbour. He threw a lifebelt attached to a rope over the stern, and the dolphin quickly surfaced beside where it splashed in the water. The boat's engine roared again and Fungie accompanied us into the harbour.

Back in calmer waters, I undressed in the wheelhouse and stuffed myself into the wetsuit. Outside on deck I put on the fins and pulled over the wetsuit hood. The dolphin was still back at the lifebelt. He had learned to expect human company there and was waiting for it to arrive. I slipped on the face mask and snorkel and sat over the side of the boat. Holding my face mask in my hand I plunged into the water.

The cold shocked me. Bubbles swirled around from the splash but they quickly raced back to the surface. Gradually my wetsuit began to warm up. I rose to the surface, took in some air and swam back towards the lifebelt. Fungie had gone. I grabbed the lifebelt and looked back to the boat. They were pointing away. Fungie had gone on; they were going to see if they could bring him back. I let go the lifebelt. While waiting I dived a few times.

I was in a dark, green, gloomy and silent world. Light disappeared into darkness in a radius ten metres away from me as if the sea had drawn across a curtain to protect its secrets. Below

I saw a pair of legs dangling in watery space. My legs. Shafts of sunlight passed them by on their way down into the ocean night. The thought that something was going to emerge from that gloom to examine me kept me alert, if not a little frightened.

I couldn't see the dolphin. I knew that if he was near he would be able to "see" me in his own way – with sound. He might even already be bouncing ultrasonic beams off the millions of tiny air bubbles enclosed within my wetsuit's skin. If I had been in ordinary swimming togs his ultrasound would have penetrated my skin and bounced off the bones in my ribcage and the air in my lungs. In any case he would know what distance I lay away from him by the gap in time between each echo. Would he think I was worth a closer inspection?

I came to the surface. The boat was about 80 metres away. The people bent over on one side provided the tell-tale sign that Fungie was with them. Then they all stood up. They were shouting and waving. A cry came down with the wind.

"He's coming back to you!"

He wasn't on the surface, so I ducked underwater. I thought I made out a blur passing far to my right. Was it a tail? A minute passed. A chilling sensation crept over me. There was a "presence" in the area. Something was out there close by, hiding in that dark wilderness. I was sure of it. The picture of a friendly dolphin had vanished and my mind was now full of prowling phantoms. I ducked down and peered hard into the gloom. Nothing. Frightened or not, I wasn't going to let any phantom take me unawares.

The cry came again: "He's right behind you!"

I ducked and looked to my right. Nothing. I looked to my left. I was staring into a large eye on a very large head! He was a giant, and he could hardly have come any closer.

I felt my hair attempting to stand up under the tight hood of my wetsuit. I took a sharp breath – which was a mistake as the snorkel was submerged and half of what I inhaled was

water. While the dolphin watched me I struggled up to the surface and tried to recover from my sudden fit of coughing. At last I got a clear breath of air and ducked down again.

His giant shape overshadowed mine as he held his position alongside me. What a creature! My nervousness was now completely gone and I reached out to try to touch him. He drew wide of my outstretched hand by twitching sideways. As he did so the watery sunbeams caught his white underbelly. He was not the dusky grey-backed creature that we had seen on the surface. He had a radiant glow. He also had a lovely wide grin.

He stayed for a while, a sympathetic, almost fatherly figure dwarfing a struggling newcomer to his world. I kicked my fins and moved ahead. He responded by gliding alongside. Our silent communication lasted for about a minute. Then, with a turn of his tail, he moved towards the boat.

Over a 20-minute spell he came back to me three times. On one visit he hung in front of me, his head cocked to one side, and he seemed to be checking me out. Then he beat his tail again and was gone. That was the end of my first underwater encounter with Fungie.

During the next few visits I grew to appreciate him as a master of stealth. Even if I spotted him some 30 metres away across the surface of the sea he had the unnerving habit of being able to appear suddenly right beside me. By chance I might look down. There, gliding eerily into view below my feet, would be the unmistakable giant form. He might choose to lie back in the water and look up at me, his white belly making him glow like an apparition. On other occasions a loud blast of air behind me would announce that he had been with me already for some time.

Once you have recovered from the shock of his presence you can admire him. He is between three-and-a-half and four metres long but the water and your face mask make him look even bigger. His scars are striking. His whole body looks like a notepad that has been scribbled on

and he gets new marks every week because a dolphin's skin is sensitive and easily scratched. The scars tell of jousts with engine propellers around which Fungie loves to weave just inches away. For every miscalculation he earns a scar.

His size and sudden appearances are the only daunting aspects about his presence. In fact, once you get to know him you see an almost comical side. He can only twitch his head slightly to the right and left – evolution got rid of the neck for a streamlined, uniform body. When you look at the round face, the stiff neck and the built-in smile you are reminded of a kindly, well-fed gentleman. When he opens his mouth and nods rapidly you might imagine that he is chortling at some private joke.

Fungie has other markings which would identify him from other dolphins. He has a dimple-like nick on his whitened lower jaw-tip and another nick on his right fluke (the flat tail-wing). A mark like a bullet hole just above his left eye was caused by a parasite called a penella. The penella burrows into the blubber and grows. This nasty piece of work was visible on Fungie during his early days in Dingle but happily it died off, leaving no lasting damage. The hole mark, too, has faded almost completely.

Fungie's watery domain allows him almost total freedom of movement. Gravity has no hold on him. He can be seen hanging upside-down monitoring a lobster's progress across the sea-bed one minute, lying on his back in midwater like a prone sunbather the next. His agility when moving is superb, his pace electric. Another of his habits, frightening at first sight, is to approach you with his mouth open, displaying neat rows of sharply pointed teeth. This usually happens when something fascinates him, a camera perhaps.

His open-mouthed gaze is a picture of boyish, joyous wonder. On one occasion he was fascinated by the frayed end of a rope I happened to be hanging on to. He moved up from underneath, almost pushing me out of his way, and took the frayed part into his mouth. He closed his mouth gently on it before releasing it. It's his way of examining texture. Other people have felt a slight grip on their legs – a rather chilling method of analysis.

If Fungie takes a liking to you he will suddenly embark on a frenzy of activity, leaping beside or even over you or else poking his head above the water and holding that position close to you. He might also circle rapidly around underwater. If you manage to touch him he accelerates as if delighting in your response.

Many people emerge from these encounters in a high state of excitement and enthusiasm. The aura around Fungie seems to be so radiant that people get "burnt" by it. One such person is Siobhán Daly, a Caherciveen girl who crossed the bay and met Fungie in June 1988. She went swimming from *Sláidín* and saw Fungie from a distance. With others in the water she felt brave; she swam further out. Suddenly he came near her. She looked down: he was looking at her! She felt the strangest sensation, as if she were seeing a vision. But, like a vision, he disappeared into the dark fathoms.

Siobhán travelled on, teaching that summer in a school in the USA, but the vision kept coming back to her. She told the children about the dolphin. They were enchanted and kept asking her to talk about him. She returned to Dingle and went out regularly to swim with him.

Many people become enraptured by Fungie. They think about nothing but dolphins for weeks afterwards. Many openly express a wish to come back as a dolphin in the next life. The dolphin is associated with happiness, its world is thought of as a distant place, an Atlantis that lies over the sea's farthest horizon. It's not hard to see why humans aspire to that kind of fantasy land. Perhaps the feeling of euphoria comes from the sense of getting a glimpse of it: for a few magic, fleeting moments in Dingle an invisible barrier between two worlds comes down. Then, all too soon, Fungie goes back to his world, leaving not a little happiness painted on the faces of those he has left behind.

DANGER

THE PEACEFUL AND friendly relationship between Fungie and human beings came under threat in the summer of 1989 when strange shadows were cast over Dingle harbour. On Saturday 17 June a tug led the way into the harbour, dragging behind it a towering suction-cutter dredger. Further behind rolled two giant barges and the dredger's platform ship. They seemed like monsters from another world, making the fishing boats at the pier look small and insignificant.

Their names came from legends of ancient Rome. The dredger was called *Mercurius* after the Roman god of commerce. One barge was *Mars*, the god of war; the other was *Pluto*, the god of the dead. *Argos*, the tug, recalled the adventures of Jason and the Argonauts. Some people, when they saw these names from classical Rome, were reminded of another Roman god, Apollo, who could turn himself into a dolphin and who was the god of light, beauty and intelligence.

These cranking modern monsters of steel with their ancient names had come to Dingle because over the years the harbour had silted badly, with the result that deep-water craft were not able to use the pier any more. The job these strange vessels were in Dingle to do would benefit the town, but one look at the cutter on the front of the *Mercurius* would make any dolphin-lover swallow hard. The teeth on the enormous drill-head would gorge sand and rock day and night for three months ahead.

Concern had been raised on radio and in the newspapers. What precautions could be taken to protect this delicate creature? His inquisitiveness alone would, it was thought, be his undoing. A pump-action shaft drill, used in the harbour on a modest operation a few months before, had caught Fungie's attention immediately and he had stayed close to the shaft during most of its

activity. But if Fungie ventured near the angry spinning head of the *Mercurius* the result would almost certainly be fatal. The rotation generated a whirlpool and anything close by would be drawn in and chewed up.

The dredging people, Holland and Company, gave assurances that no explosives, commonly used in operations like this, would be used to remove hard rock. They also assured the public that they would pay respect to Fungie and watch his movements close to the dredging. Other than that little could be done. It would be left to the gods – and Fungie's own wits.

On Sunday 18 June the dredger took up position at the harbour's mouth where it would begin dredging. I was out there at the time with Dingle man Tommy Flannery. Without warning the drill suddenly dropped below the surface. The drilling had started. There was only a gentle rippling on the surface, not the turbulence we had expected.

We looked around for Fungie but couldn't see him. He had been there earlier. In fact he had hardly left the steel hulks since they had arrived in the harbour on the previous day. We glanced at each other; Tommy shrugged his shoulders; after a while he happened to look out towards the bay. One hundred metres off, rising and sinking gently in the sun-dappled blue, was the unmistakable fin. We had been looking the wrong way: Fungie wasn't paying the slightest heed to the dredging.

The dolphin had sensibly decided to keep clear of the dangerous cutting and suction action of the dredger. From time to time he went up to the dredger's side and nuzzled at the large tyres that provided buffers, but throughout the months during which the dredger worked he gave a wide berth to its spinning teeth.

The barges, however, attracted his interest whenever they passed through the harbour's mouth. As they hauled their huge loads of rock out to sea he would position himself by the side or the

bow of the *Pluto* or *Mars* as each of them heaved its 1,000-ton load out for dumping. The great

wave that was pushed up from the sea at the bow of the barge was much bigger than any created by the much smaller craft that brought tourists out to see him. Once a barge sailed into view Fungie would be gone: the boatmen would have to start engines and give pursuit. Sometimes a barge would have one dolphin and four boatloads of tourists for company; its crew had never experienced as much attention!

One bright, cool morning the sun had not yet dissolved an early mist which cast a fine veil over the world, ghosting away from view the Iveragh peninsula across the bay. Fungie deserted the boat that I was in to follow the *Pluto* which was carrying a load out to sea. We decided to follow it and began a race with the metal hulk, ploughing alongside until we were eventually level with her bow. Except for the swathe cut by the bow in its silvery surface the sea was calm and smooth as a pool. The rush of water was loud enough to drown out the drone of our engine.

Fungie was there, where we suspected he would be, appearing about once every half-minute, rising and falling just feet in front of the barge. There was no discord, only the harmonious relationship between two travellers, a giant workhorse and its faithful friend of the sea.

THE CELEBRITY

FUNGIE IS NOT the first dolphin in modern times to become famous on account of his friendship with humans. During the 1970s the streets of Corogna in Spain were jammed at weekends with visitors coming to see a Bottlenose dolphin called Nina. Thousands of people swam into the sea to be near him. The tourist trade boomed and property prices in the small fishing town shot up. All available boats were commandeered for dolphin trips. The local council ordered all fishing nets out of the water and the use of grenades to stun and catch fish was prohibited. Nina's welfare became the official concern of the Spanish navy.

The story, however, ended sadly. Nina was found dead up against some rocks. It was winter and there were few tourists around. It seems that some of the fishermen had begun to use grenades again and that one of these had killed the dolphin. The whole community mourned and the council ordered a monument to be built in fond memory of a friend.

Opo, the female dolphin in New Zealand, so enchanted everyone that the parliament passed a law to protect it. France had its own friendly dolphin, Jean Louis (later discovered to be a female) who swam off the Brittany pensinsula. Cornwall had a male Bottlenose dolphin, Percy, in the mid-1970s, who gave joy to its citizens for almost two years. Wales had Simo, named after the famous dolphin of ancient Naples. This Welsh Simo was actually believed to be a dolphin also known as Donald who had previously patrolled around the Isle of Man.

During six years in the early 1960s a dolphin accompanied boats and attracted swimmers in Fifeshire in Scotland. In America in 1971, Dolly, a female Bottlenose dolphin, befriended the Asbury family in Florida, staying in one of the Florida Keys' canals behind their house. In May

1990 I visited Joce, a friendly female dolphin in Kotor, Yugoslavia. The encounter was fleeting but memorable: Joce travelled right up to the pier and promptly turned on her back to allow a group of children to pet her. The Turks and Caicos Islands in the British West Indies have Jo Jo while, a little closer to home, Freddie swims off the English harbour town of Amble in Northumberland. The stories of all these dolphins are similar: the first tentative contact, the experience of friendship and gentleness, and then an increasing number of people going out to meet him.

In Dingle Fungie was only beginning to be famous in 1987. One boat was regularly taking people out on day trips to see him, and one boat was enough to cater for the numbers. In late October that year the *Oireachtas*, the annual festival of Irish culture, began in the town. On the weekend before its opening the open-air public address system crackled a message across the town: one-hour trips to see Fungie the Dingle dolphin were departing from the pier. The first boat was joined by another the following day, and dolphin-watching was about to become a minor industry in Dingle.

News stories about Fungie began with a trickle in the local newspapers, dwelling mainly on the fact that Fungie was without a mate. The stories fanned the interest of the national newspapers. One of the first major features, including close-up pictures of Fungie underwater, appeared in the *Sunday Press*, written by Ronan Quinlan, a photographer with the *Press* group. Ronan was also a diving colleague of Ronnie Fitzgibbon and had joined him in his adventures with Fungie. Many of those underwater pictures were to appear later in Ronnie's book, *The Dingle Dolphin*, which itself contributed to the dolphin's growing popularity.

Fungie made his first appearance on Irish television at the end of 1987 as part of a Christmas quiz in *To the Waters and the Wild*, the wildlife programme made by Gerrit van Gelderen. The film shown during the quiz had been shot in July when Gerrit, a frequent visitor to Dingle,

had been told about Fungie by local friends and had gone out to the harbour's mouth to find him.

"I remember it was a very calm day. We eventually found him in one of the caves," recalls Gerrit. "He was lying quite still, his head sticking above the water, either relaxing or sleeping." Gerrit moored the boat in front of the cave and his son Merlin and friend Paul slipped into the water with a camera. The activity startled the dolphin and he swam away at first. But the camera intrigued him. He came back.

"He stuck his nose right up against the lens – we couldn't get him away from it," says Gerrit. "We couldn't use most of the shots because all that appeared was a huge snout pressed against the glass." But eventually enough suitable film was shot and the programme went out. In his commentary Gerrit did not pinpoint the dolphin's whereabouts: "I thought that the more tourists that came to visit him the less chance there was that he would stay."

However, the growing attention didn't seem to worry the dolphin. The first full feature film on Fungie was made by dolphin film-maker and author Dr Horace Dobbs. Promoting his theory that dolphins help relieve depression in humans, Dr Dobbs brought three people from England to meet Fungie. The film, *The Dolphin's Touch*, was shown on ITV in 1988 as part of a series called *The Human Factor*. The reaction to the film was instant and soon Fungie the local hero had become Fungie the international celebrity.

After *The Dolphin's Touch* several more television crews arrived. RTE, BBC, Sky TV and ITV all made programmes, and the reaction to BBC's *Blue Peter* showing him was particularly good.

His celebrity travelled across the Atlantic when American television broadcast features on him in the USA. Australia's Channel 9 compared him with their own dolphins who regularly swim near the shoreline in Monkey Mia in Western Australia. On one occasion Fungie bathed a French TV film crew with the splash from one of his big jumps. Dutch, German and Japanese

television film crews all made the trip to Dingle to see and film Ireland's friendly dolphin. Matthew Collins, a reporter for BBC's *The Travel Show*, rated his time with Fungie in Dingle as the best of all his worldwide travels, thus contributing to a resurgence of British tourism to Dingle. Brenda Greene, who worked on *The Travel Show*, recalled that such was the interest after the broadcast that a special standard letter about Fungie and Dingle had to be printed up in order to answer all the enquiries they received.

The trickle of newspaper articles had become a flood. Almost every major British newspaper dispatched journalists and photographers to capture the magic of Fungie. Articles appeared in the London *Independent*, the *Star*, the *Daily Mail*, *Today*, the *Times* and the *Daily Mirror*. In the US the *New York Times* and the *Washington Post* wrote long articles about Ireland's dolphin while *Hello* magazine and the *National Enquirer*, and Swedish newspaper *Expressen*, all featured the dolphin in colour spreads.

Most media coverage concentrated on the human aspect of the dolphin's relationship with people, and regularly wrote about Fungie's "loneliness" until humans befriended him. These stories overlooked the fact that Fungie had been alone, and contentedly so, during his first two years in Dingle, and that during the very stormy winter of 1989 he had to forgo human company for weeks on end. Another rather fanciful newspaper story alleged that some people in Cahirciveen, on the southern side of Dingle Bay, were involved in a plot to kidnap Fungie by enticing him across the bay with squid. The unlikelihood of this notion was pointed out by one Dingle citizen who commented: "Who's going to start throwing squid out at £1 a pound?"

The dredging of the harbour in 1989 launched dozens of stories about whether Ireland's favourite animal would be hurt by the drill. Later that same year the *Irish Press* highlighted concern by some tourist interests that Fungie was exhausted by the sheer number of tourists that were travelling to see him. When explosives were used in the harbour to remove rock in

December 1989 all the Irish media focused on the threat to Fungie and the precautions taken to protect him.

His celebrity drew tourists from far and wide. When 13-year-old Aaf Verkade from Nymegen in Holland broke her leg in a skiing accident, her parents asked her where she would like to go as a treat when she recovered. Aaf promptly produced one of the Dutch national newspapers and pointed at a picture of Fungie. Arriving in Dingle, Aaf was very nervous at the prospect of meeting a wild dolphin; she had only met dolphins in aquariums before. But this was where she had wanted to be, and there was no turning back.

"I was in the water and I thought my foot was resting on a sand-bank," she recalls. "I looked down and there he was. Fungie's nose was at my fin!"

Thrilled at the experience, Aaf was back in the water the following day.

Fungie's personality has inspired wonder in many people, one of whom was the poet and playwright Heathcote Williams who had championed the cause of whales in his world-famous poem, *Whale Nation*. Now he came to Dingle and wrote, in *Falling for a Dolphin*, about the adventure of getting to know Fungie:

> And your mind feels recharged by the nameless wildness of this creature,
> So stretched that you effortlessly think of it as a person,
> Of your two minds blending,
> Your mind reaching out and becoming one with another.

FUN AND GAMES

OUR BOAT WAS out early one fresh September morning. We spent a fruitless half-hour searching coves and inlets and scanning the horizon for Fungie.

"They mustn't have blown him up yet for today," said one passenger, voicing the popular joke that in someone's shed each night lay a deflated dolphin dummy with a little two-cylinder engine strapped underneath.

Fungie obviously had better things to do than to visit our boat. Perhaps a shoal of fish had excited him and he had gone fishing. We turned back, but as we approached the mouth of the harbour we saw him. What had grabbed his interest was a group of canoes paddling just off the shore.

He was being playful, standing up out of the water beside each canoe in turn. But then he seemed to take a liking to one canoeist in particular. She kept turning away from him but that did not deter Fungie. Like a swimmer trying to get on board, he raised himself up out of the water and laid his body across the canoe. The woman didn't like it: Fungie was being a bit too forward for her; so she paddled closer to land. Fungie followed at first but then he gave up. After all, there were plenty of other canoes in the sea. A small one with a large man on board caught his attention and he swam around it, nosing it as if to test its texture. The man had only a baseball bat for a paddle.

Fungie dived and reappeared, rose up in the water and laid himself across the end of the canoe. Then he kicked a few times with his tail and moved speedily through the water, leaving **72/** one surprised and dizzy man rotating in his canoe, a helpless rider on an unexpected merry-go-

round. It was difficult to resist the impression that Fungie's open-mouthed expression was a big, broad smile.

Soon a much larger canoe came into sight and Fungie was up to it in a second. He prepared himself as before but, no matter how hard he kicked, the canoe refused to budge. It was obvious that he was straining with all his might and the people watching from the boats couldn't help laughing.

There is a spark in Fungie, a lively inquisitiveness that leads him to play in many different ways. He does not play with everyone who goes to meet him; sometimes he just does not seem to be in the mood. But anyone who spends much time with him soon finds that he is an extremely playful character.

All kinds of different things can catch his attention and become the starting point for a game. It might be something as small as a medallion being rubbed along its chain, or the winding of a waterproof watch – both sounds which he can hear clearly underwater – or the brush of your wetsuit against his skin. Suddenly he starts making rapid movements around you, a tell-tale sign of what is to come. Then he explodes into full-blown play. He might suddenly leap out of the water and over you, or he might stand right up out of the water, nodding his head, just beside you.

The play falls into routines. He will swim around and close to you but dodge away when you try to touch him. He will still keep swimming around, however. He knows you are trying to touch him; it seems as if he's trying to egg you on, to dare you to catch him. When he circles he is at the frontier of his own world, the wild, which he does not cross willingly by touching you. Yet he seems to will humans to do it. The challenge has been thrown down. The game is on.

It is rather one-sided because Fungie's speed gives him a definite advantage. When you have

to keep turning around in the water to keep him in view, you soon get exhausted. If, however,

you happen to have an extension to your arm such as a paddle you may be able to surprise him by catching him at his nearest orbit and gently prodding his side.

The touch causes Fungie to accelerate around you and then, a few times during every complete circle, he raises his head up out of the water and back down again. This game of touch, which happens frequently, usually has one ending. The human withdraws to go back to the boat, tired and very dizzy.

Fungie often tries to touch paddles. Canoeists who know this let their paddles lie flat just above the water if Fungie is below them. Seeing the blade the dolphin may come up and touch it. The canoeist then raises his paddle into the air slightly and Fungie will often raise himself up to touch it again. The paddle is raised higher and the dolphin rises higher. Sometimes Fungie is almost standing out of the water and the paddle is at arm's length in the air.

The dolphin is a large, heavy and powerful animal and his antics can sometimes be a little dangerous to those around him. People who go out in small boats should know that Fungie doesn't play by any rules. He may try to capsize them, as he has often done to windsurfers, mounting the board and causing the surfer to lose balance. It can seem at times as if Fungie thinks anyone who does not actually get into the water with him is not playing fair. Any craft he is able to turn runs the risk of being capsized. Even a speeding inflatable may sometimes receive a knock from him directly underneath; if this doesn't work he may move ahead and try to divert it from its course.

Anything new is likely to appeal to him. A football or inflated toy often gets a good going over. Once Fungie had half an hour of continuous fun following a pink inflated dolphin as it hung by a rope from a boat. It would skim the water then suddenly shoot into the air as if punched by some invisible force. Then Fungie would reveal himself, lunging up from underneath, and carrying it for a split second on his back before the toy was yanked away from him by the pull of the rope.

Not to be outdone, Fungie would dart ahead of it, wait, and bat it up again. The next day he ignored the inflated dolphin completely: its novelty value had gone.

He does not need manufactured objects or human beings to be playful. His continuous fun with cormorants when on his own has been witnessed by many. Jim McKenna of Dingle watched from the shore as Fungie created a fuss around one such sea-bird. "The cormorant took off to get away from him," recalls Jim. "It flew a hundred yards and landed. But the dolphin just came out of the water right beside it. It had obviously sped after it, watching its flight from underwater." The cormorant flew off again but again Fungie popped up as if by magic at the bird's landing spot. "The cormorant could get no peace that time," added Jim.

Another game that comes naturally to Fungie is tossing fish. On a day when the harbour's mouth was calm as glass we saw him in the distance lolling on his back, his pectoral fin-tips pointing up into the air. As he turned over we noticed he had a small fish, a pollock, in his mouth. He let it drop into the water a few times. Then, taking it in his mouth again, he suddenly whipped his head skywards. The fish shot into the air. It plopped back into the water beside him. He picked it up. The pollock shot skywards again. This went on for several minutes, Fungie watching the airborne fish with idle curiosity, like a cowboy flicking a dime.

Word got about one summer that Fungie enjoyed listening to music. An article in the *Daily Mail* claimed that he had been captivated by the sounds of the tune "Dingle Bay" being played on a tin whistle. As if to prove it, a large centre-spread picture accompanying the story showed Fungie standing high out of the water in front of a player sitting on a dinghy.

The idea was not new. Two thousand years ago the Roman scholar Pliny wrote that dolphins were susceptible to the charm of music, and the dolphin-god, Apollo, the god of light, was also the god of music. Soon passengers on the dolphin boats were competing with each other for Fungie's attention with tin whistles, flutes, recorders, mouth-organs and even a trumpet.

Fungie seemed to respond – not to all overtures, but to some – and on a few occasions the music maker was rewarded by the dolphin rising out of the water extremely close by. One elderly couple from England had their parts rehearsed. The woman had changed into swimwear and stood ready at the side of the boat. At the first approach of Fungie she rapped out the order, "play it." Her husband responded with the opening strains of "The Banks of My Own Lovely Lee" on his mouth organ. The melody didn't succeed too well, for Fungie only came over to the woman when the tune was finished!

Most people go out just to see Fungie, not necessarily to see him jumping or performing. If they do they may well be disappointed. He is not a plaything but a wild, free creature of the sea. He can and will play whenever and wherever the mood takes him. For his human visitors it is a bonus simply to be there when he does.

JUMPING FOR JOY

NATURE IS FULL of spectacular sights. The flight of an eagle, the gallop of a wild horse, the dive of a gannet – these are just three of the thousands of exciting sights of the natural world. But few such sights are as dramatic as the jump of a dolphin. And Fungie is a wonderful jumper. For one, breathtaking instant he cuts from his own world, shooting through the surface like a bolt from the blue. He can climb as high as four metres in the air, and sometimes he will launch himself through the air at terrific speed, clearing a distance of ten or 15 metres.

Taking off vertically out of the water, he turns almost casually at the top of his jump to make a head-first re-entry. He performs a cross-leap, jumping first in one direction and then back again immediately. He does mid-air twists, loops, and back-flips. No one can ever predict which way he will jump next. For this is a wild creature, not a trained performer.

It is in the hope of seeing such aerobatics that people crowd *Sláidín* at the mouth of Dingle harbour or go out in flotillas of leisure boats during the height of summer. Some people believe that Fungie doesn't just jump to please himself. Retired Dingle fisherman Tom Kennedy speaks of the "salute" the dolphin gives to many of his regular visitors in fishing boats.

"We would be coming in from some lobster fishing in our small boat. Fungie would be alongside. Then when we were moving into shallower waters in Dingle harbour the dolphin would start going under the boat and trying to lift it up."

Tom feels Fungie was trying to put a brake on the boat's progress up the harbour and beyond his own limits. "When he realized that wouldn't work and we crossed beyond his mark he would give one big leap behind. It's his way of saying 'Goodbye, I'll see you again'."

Another fisherman, Michael Sheehy, skipper of the *Silver Fern*, has also witnessed Fungie's special jumping displays. "We were sailing out one evening. Fungie was with three small boats just off *Sláidín* strand. He went up to the first boat and did five jumps in circular movements alongside. Then he moved onto the next boat and did five wheels again. He did the exact same number of jumps beside all the boats."

Fungie's jumping, spectacular as it may often be, is not an everyday occurrence. Sometimes he might lie low for two or three whole weeks. Then, suddenly, he might start throwing himself into the air with so many leaps one after the other that anyone watching would almost think that the sea had become boiling hot.

He also jumps over humans, picking his exit and entry spots in the water exactly, so that he passes close but does not hit the swimmer. Kevin McCulloch is a quiet-spoken man from Surrey in England who heard about the dolphin and travelled to Dingle to see him. On the first day there his mile-long walk out to *Sláidín* was fruitless: the day was windy and wet and he saw nothing. Later that afternoon he took a boat out. At least he saw him this time but Fungie was in a quiet mood, hardly visible beneath the waves. His third trip, the following day, saw events change dramatically.

"A man at the pier said Fungie was in a jumping mood that day. I had no idea how he knew, but I went out with expectation. Our boat trailed a lifebelt at the end of a rope. I was in a wetsuit so I slipped overboard, swam to it and hung on. The boat was moving and causing turbulence. Fungie seemed to be attracted by it. He swam by my side. With my goggles on I could look at him looking at me under the water. Then he decided to jump. . ."

They were rare jumps. Fungie took off on one side, flew high over the swimmer and plunged in on the other side. He repeated the jump again and again for a full five minutes, a long time in anybody's life when a great creature weighing a quarter of a ton is crossing over you. Kevin

claims to have felt completely safe throughout the experience.

"It wasn't frightening. I knew he was friendly and felt sure he could judge a safe distance from me to come down. All the same, it seemed very close."

A DOLPHIN'S LIFE

A DOLPHIN MOVES away from a herd. She has been carrying her young in her womb for nearly a year and is about to give birth. Another adult female dolphin, one with no young herself, breaks from the herd to give assistance.

The young dolphin or calf emerges tail first. If the head came first and the birth was delayed by a few vital seconds it would drown. As soon as the head appears the mother and the "aunt" turn to the newborn dolphin and rush it towards the surface for its first lungful of air.

It is a male, about one metre in length, over a quarter the size of its mother. Like his mother he's an Atlantic Bottlenose dolphin. He has the same colouring: his slate-grey back blends with the sea's surface tones, while his underbelly matches the white sky and makes the dolphin almost undetectable to any prey or predator below him. The dolphin's mother has been weakened by the birth so another female comes to support her while the first attendant nudges the young dolphin above the surface.

Both parent and offspring are all right, and soon comes the first feeding. The young dolphin finds the mother's two teats just below her belly. He presses against one of them. His straight hard jaw cannot suck from the teat; instead the mother, sensing his touch, sends jets of warm milk into his mouth.

The young dolphin is already fully developed. His head and body are the same shape as an adult's, only smaller. The thick layer of blubber beneath his skin protects him from the cold water and keeps him buoyant. It will act as a food store if ever he faces a period of hunger.

He can swim right from birth, stroking his tail up and down and using the two pectoral fins on his side for steering. His little body has to flap quickly and furiously to keep up with his mother's bigger, more powerful strokes. She will not travel too far or too fast with her young calf, however. And when they have to go on long treks with the herd she will keep him just behind or below her pectoral fin – or flipper – so that her own swimming will also carry him along. If he falls out of this vital slipstream he will quickly exhaust himself by being forced to swim constantly, and he may die. Many young and inexperienced mothers lose their young this way. But he is lucky: his mother trains him well to keep station by her side.

The young dolphin is in a herd of 20 other dolphins. His own sub-group consists of mothers and their young, the family unit within the herd. Dolphins aged three years or more have broken off to form a sub-group of their own. Other dolphins, some as old as eight or nine, are still accompanying their mothers; one old female has two generations of her young swimming with her. Adult males remain apart from the females. Sometimes whole herds are composed only of adult males.

From the time of his birth the mother caresses and strokes her young dolphin gently and continually, teaching him to respond by touch. He learns to recognize other dolphins by touch. When playing with them he will bump and rub against them, flap his flippers on theirs and nip and rake their sides with his teeth. He will even turn around to touch their tail fluke with his own. As he grows older he will play endlessly with any curiosity for the pleasure of its touch on his smooth, sensitive skin. Often he will try to carry a twig or a live turtle on top of his head or nudge them along with his beak, treating them as playthings. Touching and stroking will have an important role later on in courtship and mating.

The dolphin is born into a world of sound. The sea, the weather, and other sea creatures all make noises around him, much of which he finds strange and sometimes frightening at first.

He hears other dolphins and whales whistling and calling. He soon learns to recognize the

special whistle made by his mother as his own identity call or name. And he will recognize not only his mother but his older sisters, aunts and grandmother by the slight variations in their whistle calls, all of which echo the whistle call of his great-grandmother, the founder of this female band.

As he grows older he will come to know other males and females outside his family by their special calls, though at times his sharp sense of taste can lead him to his mother or other dolphins he knows without even calling. The young dolphin will also learn to use body language, adopting positions in the water to show his feelings or to indicate what he wants to do.

If he should ever not heed his mother's call or if he steps out of line she will reprimand him with a sharp nip, a bump with her jaw, or even a thump of her tail. He may have wandered too far away from the herd, curious about another marine creature. For this he gets a jab in the side as his mother leads him quickly back to the group. Mothers are always trying to keep their young in order, though the older mothers are more relaxed and tolerate more wandering and rough play. Together the females keep an eye on all the herd's young and are quick to retrieve them if danger threatens. Many dolphins, young and old, bear scars from close encounters with sharks.

If hunting sharks approach, the band draws together, guarding its young in the middle. If there is no blood in the water, coming perhaps from wounds or from feeding on fish, the sharks may pass on. If they do attack the older females may return the assault, charging the sharks with their beaks. Swimming at full speed they can punch a hole in a shark's body or break its back.

A more ominous predator is the Killer whale, also a member of the dolphin species. Some Killer whale groups hunt dolphins, sneaking up on a herd and rushing in to grab one of its members. Other Killer whale groups are fish eaters though, and dolphins can tell that they are safe to swim with.

The herd supports each of its members. If there is a sick or weak dolphin in the herd he or she is helped to the surface by other dolphins and the herd will remain in the area. The herd cannot stay forever, though, and will move on. Another dolphin may stay behind to aid the ill one, but if he does not improve the other dolphin will go back to the herd, leaving the sick dolphin to fend for itself. The mother of a young dolphin, injured, killed or caught in fishing gear, will stay with it for a long time, but she too will go back to the group eventually.

The young dolphin's community has no leader. His own female band is the most permanent group but even senior females move off for short periods. Adult males wander alone sometimes, in search of a female to mate with; the younger males hunt for females in groups. Some male dolphins visit neighbouring communities looking for mates and may join the new group for days or even years. But even those lone, male dolphins which have wandered furthest afield will return from time to time to be with their family herd.

While there is no dominant dolphin in the herd, dolphins of all ages and sexes have disputes. But, after chasing and snapping, the winner is decided without much injury to either side. Serious fights could end in real injury, but these are very rare.

The young dolphin and his mother follow the herd as it travels the Atlantic along the coastal shores of western Europe, visiting bays and inlets on route. If the fish stocks are good the herd will stay a while before moving on. Dolphin herds establish territories spanning a 100 kilometre range. Sometimes they may meet other dolphins who have made their home in a bay.

After feeding the dolphins may bask and play or explore the area. If the dolphins spot a fishing boat they may race to join up with it. The dolphins queue in order of seniority to take turns at riding the wave at its strongest point – near to the boat's bow. The wave gives their skin a massage as well as providing a push. An eager young dolphin who tries to slip into the queue

may be caught by its mother and ushered quickly away. Dolphins do not have to find a boat to ride a bow wave – a large whale can be just as good. The herd may also race big waves towards the shoreline, much to any human surfer's surprise.

In a large fishing ground the young dolphin's herd may be joined by more herds, swelling their numbers to several hundred. He will not be allowed to hunt until he is bigger; for now he is left with other dolphins while his mother joins the hunt. Afterwards the giant herd breaks up into the smaller original herds. Each one may have gained or lost dolphins to another.

A herd does not have to join up only with other dolphins. The young dolphin may at some time find himself accompanying a herd of Pilot whales, large dark creatures with bulbous heads. Despite their difference in colour and size, he feels at home among them. They too have several generations of females and their young, just like his mother's band.

After two years the dolphin is weaned off his mother's milk. He has already grown teeth at the age of six months – between 72 and 104 of them in all – shaped like pegs and with single roots. His mother introduces him to live small fish – he does not eat dead fish. He swallows them whole, using his teeth not for chewing but for holding his food. His two stomachs break the toughest of chunks down into nutrients for his growing body.

He now learns to participate in the fish hunt in earnest. The first member of the herd to discover a shoal of fish gives the alert, jumping into the air or communicating with calls. The rest of the herd then spreads out and tries to surround or shepherd the shoal towards shallow waters; there the fish become confused and easier to manage.

While two dolphins stand sentry on either side, keeping the shoal squeezed in a ball, the rest of the herd take turns at going in and picking off a fish. The young dolphin waits his turn, then flashes forward, sweeping up a specimen. He may attack the shoal several times until finally it is the sentry's turn. The remainder of the shoal is released.

As he grows older his skills of hunting and swimming become sharper. One day he may decide to leave the herd and explore. Dolphins frequently roam on their own or become independent of a herd. He will travel leisurely through the water, disappearing under the surface and emerging long distances away to spout air. He can accelerate dramatically. Unlike a fish, which twists its tail sideways, the dolphin's upward tail-stroke drives him through the water, the downward beat returning it for the next drive forward. At full speed, close to 30 kilometres an hour, the stroke movement is smaller but faster. He bends his tail flukes in subtle movements while swimming so that he can pass smoothly through the water with the least disturbance. He takes long leaps over the water's surface to breath in air and break from the water's energy-wasting drag. These techniques and his streamlined shape make the dolphin one of the most efficient swimming machines on this planet.

When entering an unknown area such as an estuary he moves carefully, being sure to remember exactly where he is going so that he will find his way back. He feels and tastes the water to find out if it is of the kind where he has found fish before. Then he stops and listens for sounds of food – or danger.

He turns on his sonar, a series of high-frequency emissions of pulses or click-sounds. The clicks are entirely different to the whistles he makes when he is calling other dolphins. They are made by muscles near the front of the skull and then focused through the melon, the round-shaped dome at the top of the dolphin's head. Like someone flashing a torch into a dark hall, he sweeps the area with ultrasonic beams, covering every possible angle by swimming in a figure of eight.

Echoes from his own soundings come back to him. He collects them through his lower jaw, which acts as a sound antenna and passes them to his inner ear and on to his brain. The brain translates the echoes into images. The dolphin now "sees" a rock formation 300 metres ahead, he knows the depth to the sea-bed and how far the shoreline is from him, and he recognizes the presence of a fish shoal a few hundred metres to his right.

He chases the shoal. His sonar accelerates in frequency – up to 1,000 pulses a second – as it homes in on the target, telling the dolphin that it is the kind he can eat. He is operating two sound-beams simultaneously now: one guides him to the fish; the other, a louder pulse series, keeps him informed about the area at large.

Some of the fish freeze as the hunter bears down on them. They are swept up easily. He catches one big fish and takes it to the surface where he starts to bash it against the water to break it into smaller chunks. He will have digested the fish, including its tough bones, within an hour.

The dolphin turns off his sonar and finds that the area is alive with sound anyway. Marine creatures are making defiant noises to protect their territory while other fish make mating calls. Their din leads him to more food. Altogether he eats about seven kilograms, his average intake for a day. In cold water he eats more, in warm water less.

He surfaces for air, turns and plunges back down towards the sea-bed. As he goes down his heartbeat drops from 80 to about 40 beats a minute. His rib-cage collapses slightly to allow for the increased pressure and air is compressed out of his lungs into his nasal tubes. After examining the bottom he rises, needing to take in air after six minutes. The dolphin can, however, dive to a depth of 600 metres and stay underwater for up to 15 minutes if no food is available on shallower dives.

Reaching the surface the dolphin takes short, quick intakes of air, his heartbeat accelerating to 80 beats a minute. He starts jumping high out of the water as he often does after feeding. On other occasions he jumps when he has acquired unwanted guests such as skin parasites or sea-lice. He will leap up and crash against the water in an attempt to dislodge them. The dolphin also jumps to get his bearings, spot schools of fish, or to intimidate an adversary by crashing loudly on the water. This time, though, he jumps for fun.

After a while he rests. Although he is still swimming his breathing becomes more regular and he makes no sound. He is asleep – or slumbering. Half of his brain is closed down to rest, but the other side is still alert. Otherwise he would drown. After about three hours the other side of his brain gets its turn to sleep.

The next day he is about to leave the inlet when he hears the whistle of another dolphin. He makes his own whistle. Soon a group of dolphins arrive, all whistling their calls. He does not recognize any of the group: they are young dolphins from another community out exploring. They start to imitate each other's whistles and swim together, but after a while he leaves them to return to his own community.

When he reaches ten or eleven years of age he will be fully grown, measuring some four metres in length and weighing 200 kilograms. He will also have reached sexual maturity, and will look for a mate. Some females may not accept his advances, turning their white bellies away in a sign of rejection. When he finds a partner the two will stroke, nip and bite each other and adopt elaborate postures and dance-like swimming routines. Mating itself lasts less than a minute and may be repeated several times before the dolphins go their separate ways.

For the rest of his life the dolphin will hunt, play and mate. Each day of that life he faces death from several dangers. He may become ill. If so he will seek out special foods that may cure him. A storm can upset his navigation and cause him to become stranded on shore. If he survives a stranding he risks developing pneumonia as a result of being out of the water. He faces danger from parasites, some of which would burrow into his organs, causing such pain that he might beach himself voluntarily. The dolphin could develop cancer, be hit by a boat while resting, or eat a plastic bag which blocks his digestive system and kills him. The fish he eats can bring disease if they are full of the poisonous chemicals poured into the sea by humans. He could also drown by being caught in one of the thousands of fishermen's

gill-nets which spread like cobwebs along the coastlines – his hunting ground.

If he survives he could live to a natural age of 20 years, the normal life-span of a Bottlenose dolphin, and with luck and good health he might live a few years longer. Female dolphins live to the age of 26 years and more. In his old age his body will be covered with scratches, a diary of a long, active life of courtship, hunting and sea battles. He will lose his teeth and his beak which began to turn white as he matured will now be fully white. He may start to suffer from arthritis. The dolphin's decline will be hastened when he is no longer able to catch enough fish to survive. The creature who was top of his food chain will then become food for somebody else.

SECRETS OF THE SEA

FUNGIE'S ADOPTED HOME stands at a crossroads between two marine worlds. Here sea creatures carried up by the Gulf Stream from the warm tropical waters far away to the south meet other sea creatures which have been pushed down from the cold Arctic areas to the north. We seldom see these foreigners but sometimes chance lends a hand – a rare octopus gets tangled in a fisherman's nets or a turtle is found lying on a beach, exhausted after a long trip from the Americas.

For nearly 100 years some very special people have made sure that the most interesting visitors to the shores of the Dingle peninsula have been recorded. Michael Long was the Harbour Master in Dingle when his interest in sea life led him to write detailed notes about the wealth of creatures that came to his notice. He would then pass on the information to the Natural History Museum in Dublin. Later his son, who was also called Micheal and who also became Harbour Master, carried on the custom, contributing a tremendous amount of material to the marine display section of the museum. Fishermen called into his pub at the head of the pier where they were given £1 for a rare fish find, ten shillings (50p) if it was scarce, and five shillings (25p) if it was just unusual. This reward money – which was, of course, worth an awful lot more in those days – was passed on by a fisheries inspector, and if a find was especially interesting it was mentioned in the local newspapers.

Eleven years ago Kevin Flannery inherited the tradition established by the Longs. An officer of the Department of the Marine responsible for the Clare/Kerry region, he lives in Dingle. A

phone-call to his home or a knock on his door at any hour of the day or night can result in him hurrying down to the pier to look at some rare species lying on the deck of a trawler. He carefully notes each specimen and sends its details to the Natural History Museum in Dublin and to marine centres abroad.

Foremost amongst the rare and wonderful Dingle discoveries was a cousin of the dolphin, a porpoise, which was caught accidentally in the nets of the *Roving Swan*. It is quite common for porpoises to get caught in fishing nets and drown, but this was no ordinary porpoise. It was pure white, an Albino porpoise, the only one of its kind ever to have been caught anywhere in the world. A fibre-glass replica was made and this can now be seen outside Mrs Murphy's woollen shop in Dingle.

Dolphins have on several occasions stranded themselves on the shores of the Dingle peninsula. One late call on Kevin's phone came from Tom Mitchel, who works with the Irish language radio station, *Raidio na Gaeltachta*, in nearby Ballydavid. He had been in a pub when some tourists had walked in saying they had seen a dolphin stranded in Ventry harbour.

They found the three-metre male Common dolphin in poor shape. Well-meaning attempts by people to return him to the sea by dragging him backwards had resulted in a broken right pectoral fin. (The correct way would have been to have raised him onto a blanket or coat so that his weight was spread evenly and then carried him gently to the water.) "When we launched him into the water he simply circled around," says Kevin. More than 20 times they put him into the sea, but he kept beaching himself again and later he died.

A beaching with a happier outcome took place in the Magharees on the north side of the peninsula. A Common dolphin was discovered by Pat Browne, a fisherman whose beach walks have proved a salvation for many sea species. This time the dolphin was uninjured.

Beached mammals which are returned to the water often beach themselves again within minutes. Sometimes whole herds beach together, or a dolphin may follow its stranded partner onto a beach. It is one of the great mysteries about whales and dolphins. One explanation suggests that parasites which get inside the creature cause such pain that the dolphin "commits suicide" by coming out of the sea. But what prompts whole herds to strand? A herd of Pilot whales, the species most prone to stranding, found a dry grave on Brandon beach on the north side of the peninsula in 1968, but no one knows why.

Some scientists believe that magnetic forces in local rock formations confuse their sophisticated navigation system. Kevin Flannery feels that this may be true, and he tried his own experiment with the Magharees dolphin. Together with Pat Browne and a friend, Tim Fitzgerald, they put the stranded mammal into a trailer and drove him further along the peninsula. When released back into the water the dolphin darted straight out to sea. So it may, indeed, have been magnetic interference that had caused the problem in this case. And now, somewhere in the Atlantic is a dolphin that once toured the Dingle peninsula in the back of a Land Rover!

When another Common dolphin was washed up lifeless in Dingle harbour, some fingers were pointed accusingly at Fungie. However, male dolphins are not known to fight for supremacy, and though a nasty wound near this dolphin's head suggested a violent clash, there was no evidence as to what had caused it.

One of the more distinguished visitors to Dingle Bay is the Orca or Killer whale. A member of the dolphin family, it is said to be the most intelligent of all sea species. This black-and-white-patterned giant grows to some ten metres in length and can weigh up to eight tons. It is an opportunistic eater and there is little in the way of food that it will not devour. A fully grown whale needs to eat at least three seals a day, and during the seal breeding season Killer whale pods congregate around the Blasket islands, where the seals breed. In Patagonia, South America, Killer whales lunge onto the shore to grab seals and drag them back into the water; in Arctic waters they tip over small ice-floes to get at their prey. So terrified of Killer whales are the seals

Kevin Flannery with whale skull

that some fishermen will tell you that they have been known to jump onto boats fishing around the Blasket islands in an attempt to get away from their mortal enemy.

One August afternoon in 1986 Tom Curran was fishing between *Tearaght* and *Inis Tuaisceart* islands. "I was waiting to bring up the nets when between five and ten Killer whales swam up beside the boat," Tom recalls. "Then they began to circle around it."

Being encircled by Killer whales was a new and unnerving experience for the crew. In a moment of panic Tom picked something off the deck of the boat and threw it at one of the calves among the group. It missed and the little one shot away. But the mood of the whales changed. "One of the bigger whales, probably the mother, swam straight towards us. She hit us straight amidships."

The 40-foot trawler shuddered and the lights in the wheelhouse were cut off. Tom made for the wheelhouse in order to try to steam ahead when the whale rammed again. This time the angry mother hit the rudder. "The steering was full to port and the whale pushed it completely starboard," says Tom, marvelling at this feat of strength which sent the ship's wheel spinning. They waited nervously for another ramming, but none came. The boat headed slowly back to port.

But not all the rare and unusual sea creatures that come to the coast of the Dingle peninsula are as big as whales, dolphins or porpoises. One rare warm-water visitor was a Puffer fish, a tough, prickly customer. It defends itself against predators by puffing up like a balloon. If that fails it will leave whoever eats it with a lethal belly-ache, because its organs contain a toxin about 500 times more powerful than cyanide. In Japan, Fugu, as it is called, is treated as a tasty, dangerous delicacy with only especially trained chefs licensed to prepare it in paper-thin slices. The Puffer is also known as the Voodoo fish: the black magic that makes people go into trances is believed to come from a taste of the Puffer.

Another unusual catch was one very large octopus. Kevin was intrigued when he saw it first. "It just looked like a mass of jelly with tentacles. Its eyes were three inches in diameter, its tentacles three feet long and each suction pad one inch in diameter." The pictures and details Kevin posted to marine experts in Britain and Ireland drew a blank. Nobody knew what species it was. Finally he learned from a Russian scientist that it was an extremely rare deep-water octopus.

Another visiting duo were a Remora and a Leatherback turtle. The Remora is a hitch-hiking fish which attaches itself to any larger fish by means of a flat, oval suction disc on top of its head. "In the West Indies a fisherman would tie a string onto a Remora and let him go. Five minutes later he would tug in the Remora who would by then have stuck onto a turtle." The Dingle example had hitched a ride on the world's largest turtle specimen, the Leatherback. "This one was quite a heavyweight," says Kevin. They can also live up to a century-and-a-half. "Our fellow could have floated by Napoleon's ship."

The most famous sea turtle to visit the peninsula was Timmy. Again it was Pat Browne who discovered this Loggerhead turtle and contacted Kevin. A young reddish-brown specimen, it was in poor condition, which was hardly surprising for it was thousands of miles from its North American home.

Kevin contacted the Natural History Museum in Dublin and the Northern Ireland Aquarium in Portaferry, Co. Down. Aer Lingus flew its travel-weary passenger from Farranfore airport in Kerry to Dublin. There an Air Corps helicopter picked it up and flew it to Portaferry. Aer Lingus offered to fly it first class to New York but the US would not accept one of its own for quarantine reasons. When fully recuperated, Timmy was flown by British Airways to London and then took a Portuguese Airways flight to the Madeiras where, as far as we know, he now still lives.

It was Kevin who reported the fishermen's first sighting of Fungie off Bull Head, east of *Binn Bán*, to the Natural History Museum in November 1983. And he adds a story, one that should interest the citizens of a certain harbour town in Co. Cork.

"For two years during the late '70s and early '80s boats entering Kinsale harbour were accompanied by a dolphin," says Kevin. "It rested off the main harbour buoy. Colm O'Riordan, then the Keeper of the Natural History Museum, sent me photos of this dolphin for comparisons when Fungie appeared in Dingle. I cannot say for sure, but that dolphin was not too unlike Fungie. We can never say. Nobody ever swam with the Kinsale dolphin."

THREAT TO DOLPHINS

THE STORY OF Fungie is a happy one, a story of friendship between humans and a creature of the sea. In Dingle people have for a few years been able to meet a dolphin and that encounter has helped many to understand that the world belongs to all the creatures in it, not just to human beings. Fungie now has thousands of admirers and he has become a valuable asset to tourism in the south-west of Ireland, introducing many new visitors to the beauties of the Dingle peninsula.

Sadly, though, dolphins in other parts of the world are not at all well treated by humans. In fact, human greed and thoughtlessness have created a situation in which the dolphins' world is under attack. Pollution, modern net fishing, habitat destruction, incidental capture and actual hunting have drastically reduced their numbers. Whole species that have lived undisturbed for thousands of years may be wiped out within the next 50 – because of human actions.

For a long time now the dolphins' larger cousin, the whale, has been under attack. Seven of the largest species of whales have all had their populations reduced to one-fifth of what they were at the beginning of this century. We humans are so used to thinking of whales as animals to be killed that we even named one kind the Right whale because it was the "right" whale for hunters: it swam in shallow waters, contained lots of oil and blubber, and didn't sink when it was harpooned.

Over 300,000 Blue whales were killed in the first 50 years of this century. The killing stopped in 1965 but the Blue whale, the largest creature ever to live on earth, will probably never recover from this slaughter. The Bowhead, hunted for 300 years, is now believed to number no more **/109** than 3,000, even though commercial hunting of this species stopped 70 years ago. Numbers for the Right whale are believed to be even lower.

The chief whaling nations – Iceland, Japan, Norway and the Soviet Union – were slow to heed calls that their continuous hunting would spell the end for whales. The world body that controls whaling, the International Whaling Commission, called for hunting to stop between 1986 and 1990. Japan, Norway and the Soviet Union ignored this ruling at first but finally bowed to public pressure and the threat that the US would stop buying any of their fish in 1988.

The whaling countries have tried to get around the ban, and sometimes they succeed and whales continue to die. But meanwhile a very different kind of whale industry is rapidly growing. "Whale-watching" is now a multi-million dollar industry in the United States, and other countries look likely to follow suit, including Australia, South Africa, Sri Lanka, Canada, Argentina, Mexico and New Zealand. The aim is to watch and admire these great creatures, not to harm them. For once the Grey whale's curiosity as he approaches a ship will be rewarded by a camera shot and not one from a harpoon.

As whaling has become more strictly controlled, however, the whaling countries are turning their attention towards dolphins. From the middle of the 1970s to the middle of the 1980s nearly a quarter-of-a-million dolphins were caught in Japan to be processed and sold off as meat products, including dog-food. The Dall's Porpoise, a beautiful black-and-white dolphin, has borne the brunt of the slaughter, accounting for nearly 120,000 of the quota.

The Japanese have also carried out big dolphin kills, the most notorious of which took place on Iki island during the early 1980s. The fishermen claimed that the dolphin was taking too many of the local yellowtail fish, yet not a single trace of yellowtail was found in the dolphins' stomachs. It seemed the fishermen were blaming the dolphin for their own overfishing. The slaughter brought down world condemnation on the Japanese and they stopped the killing.

Second only to Japan in the scale of dolphin hunting is Peru. This South American country had fished its stocks of anchovy, a small herring, out of existence in the 1970s. The industry then turned to dolphins, a creature which Peruvians had traditionally respected and not killed. The hunting has now grown to a stage where 10,000 Dusky dolphins, Common dolphins and Burmeister's porpoises are killed each year. Gill-net fishing is the method used but Common dolphins are also harpooned from motor-boats, an easy task since dolphins come up to the craft.

Apart from these two countries there is no large-scale hunting of dolphins. But incidental catching, where the dolphin ends up the unintended victim of the commercial fishing industry, has proved even more disastrous for the mammal. Dolphins have died in great numbers in the Eastern Tropical Pacific, which stretches from southern California to Chile and is a major fishing ground for Yellowfin tuna. In the 1960s the fishermen started using a net called the purse seine net. Drawn around a tuna shoal, the net is pulled shut at the bottom, trapping the shoal, and the catch is then hauled in.

The dolphin and the Yellowfin tuna travel together in the seas of the Eastern Tropical Pacific. Both are powerful swimmers, the tuna being one of the fastest creatures in the sea. And when the net closes around the tuna it closes around the dolphins, too. Realizing that they are trapped, the dolphins make desperate efforts to escape. But the net's transparent plastic veil confuses their echolocation system. Many try to force their way through the nets, but the more they struggle the more they become entangled. Most die from drowning. Others are crushed against the sides of boats or are smothered under the weight of tuna. Some are thrown back into the sea, their fragile flippers and dorsal fins damaged; unable to swim properly, they die lingering deaths.

Seven-and-a-half million dolphins have been killed as a result of this tuna fishing method since the 1960s. When the US government imposed heavy restrictions to try to reduce dolphin deaths the tuna industry fought the measures and succeeded in having them watered down. For a time the killing continued, but then the American people became involved on the side of the dolphins and started boycotting Yellowfin tuna. Finally, one of the two major tuna companies in America gave in and ceased buying Yellowfin caught using the method that was harmful to dolphins. Now their tins are stamped "dolphin friendly" and soon the other major company will have to do the same. But meanwhile an estimated 200,000 dolphins are killed each year in the Eastern Tropical Pacific. The numbers of the Spinner, the dolphin which got its name from its magnificent high spinning jumps, have slumped to a quarter of their original size.

Another threat to dolphins is drift-net fishing. The use all over the world of "monofilament" nets made of non-biodegradable plastic – which, in other words, will not rot away – threatens not only dolphins but all sea wildlife. These "curtains of death" can sometimes span as much as 30 miles, and within them they collect not only the fish they are hunting but also turtles, shellfish, sea-birds and other unwanted species, which end up just being thrown away. In the Gulf of California the rarest dolphin, the Vaquita, may have already disappeared from the sea, a victim of the gill-net fishing of a large fish called the totoaba.

In the North Pacific a total of 20,000 miles of drift-net is put down every day. It is estimated that up to 750,000 sea-birds are entangled in the process of salmon fishing alone. Lost nets still go on catching life until, weighed down by the sheer number of fish, mammals, sea-birds and other creatures caught in its grasp, it drifts down to the sea-bed.

We humans are so threatened by pollution in the sea that in most countries we cannot swim in the water off certain beaches. What must it be like for those that live in the sea all the time? Only recently has the world's attention been drawn to the amount of waste we pour into the seas and oceans. We dump 26,000 tons of plastic packaging into the sea each year. The world's fleet of merchant marine and naval ships drop 690,000 plastic containers into the sea each and every day. Plastic wrapping is churned out as a cheap throw-away material, but it kills marine life. Many species mistake plastic for jellyfish and become choked or poisoned by it.

Some countries' coastal waters have become like large toilets into which untreated sewage is flushed in massive amounts. The bacteria growth that results from this infects mammals, leaving lesions on their bodies. Chemicals such as PCBs (polychlorinated biphenyl), which are used in batteries and have been linked to cancer, have been discovered in young dolphins found dead on beaches in Britain. Studies indicated that they had received the poisonous chemical in their mother's milk. PCBs have also worked their way into plankton, the first rung in the food chain on which we, as fish-eating human beings, belong. What we are doing to our seas is not only killing and injuring sea creatures; it is also coming back to harm us.

The closer to modern civilization dolphins live the more they are under threat. The Yangtze River Dolphin, already in decline due to fishermen depleting its fish stocks, now faces a new threat with a proposed series of dams along its waters. The Amazon Boutu dolphin, although not as critically endangered as the Beiji, is also in decline. Recent settlers on the Amazon have been known to catch the creature to sell off its parts as fertility potions. Nearer home, on the coast of Scotland, plans for a large sewage plant threaten the grounds of one of the last surviving coastal herds of Bottlenose dolphins in the British Isles.

The facts and figures make pretty grim reading. But most people do care about the creatures who inhabit the ocean. The Amazon Boutu dolphin, for example, enjoys respect and reverence amongst the native peoples who live beside this great river. They believe that the Boutu takes the form of a handsome man at night-time and goes courting women. Unexpected pregnancies among native women have even been blamed on the Boutu! In the developed world, where tuna companies have tried to carry on killing dolphins, people-power has held back the tide of destruction.

One example of the concern that people can have for dolphins was displayed on the southern shore of Dingle Bay, in Portmagee. Veterinary surgeon Frank O'Leary was called on to help rescue a dolphin which had beached itself. When he and a colleague arrived on the shore they found the dolphin in a state of distress, calling constantly, Frank remembers, "in a way that I can only describe as a kind of keening or mourning". The men lifted the dolphin gently and returned it to the water but, once freed, he lunged back onto the beach. They pushed the dolphin out again a number of times, but with the same result. The creature seemed desperate to come on land.

Frank began to search the beach, hoping to find some clue to explain the dolphin's behaviour. In a cluster of rocks at the far end he found another dolphin; it was dead, probably killed by a boat.

The men had the dead dolphin removed, but the first dolphin's struggle towards shore continued. They called the Portmagee *garda*, Tom Clancy, for assistance. Working in turns, the three men blocked the dolphin's passage to the strand for 24 hours. Frank recalls "coming back in the morning to find Guard Clancy in his uniform, waist deep in water, pushing the dolphin back out to sea."

On the second day the dolphin gave up trying to beach itself, but it remained in the area, patrolling constantly offshore. The following day it was gone; it had, it seemed, returned to the ocean. A few days later a local farmer found the dolphin lying dead on the shore; a third dolphin was also found, beached in the same area. A small community of mammals had come to grief.

Despite its sadness, the story shows that people can act with strength and courage in an effort to save the life of a wild dolphin, and throws light on the sensitivity of a creature that arouses kindred feelings in us. Perhaps dolphins create this strong emotion because they represent the beauty and spirit of the ocean, whose mysteries and laws we have yet to understand.

FARE WELL, FUNGIE!

KNOWN TO MANY simply as "the Dingle dolphin", Fungie has built a relationship of respect and affection with the people of this historic seaport. During all the years that he has spent in Dingle he could have left at any time. Wildlife film-maker Gerrit van Gelderen feared that Fungie might go away if too many visitors came. But even after thousands have come to see him he has still remained. There is, however, always a danger that he will become a victim of his own popularity. So many people want to see him during the summer that he has to cope with eager dolphin-watchers from as early as five in the morning, and they keep on coming through the daylight hours. Only in the cold and darkness of winter does he get a rest.

One incident which taught me a lot took place in late 1989. Fungie was drifting close to a buoy. In my usual enthusiasm I stripped to my bathing-togs and jumped in from the boat. When I reached him I tried to get his attention. Fungie didn't turn around, however, as would be his normal reaction. I tried again by waving my arms. Slowly he turned around and stared at me. He didn't swim or frolic, but just looked straight at me. Then he turned back to the buoy.

The message was clear: "Go away, I want to be alone." Thinking about it afterwards, I realized that Fungie often needs to be free from the madding crowd. Fame has its price, and even for a dolphin that loves to jump and play there are times when enough is enough.

The local boatmen have the best understanding of Fungie's moods. When they realize that he doesn't want to play they will stop and watch him from a distance. Often they work together, drawing up their boats and allowing Fungie to come to them when and if he wants to. Not everyone treats Fungie with such care. Visitors in boats often persist in pursuing him, speedboats **/115** sometimes rush madly to the spot where he has started to jump – and by doing so they actually prevent him from jumping. Fungie cannot resist a chase and a speedboat gives him that challenge. It might indeed be a thrill to have a dolphin chase after you, and individually speedboat owners mean no harm, but the sheer numbers of motorized machines, particularly in the high summer, must raise the question of whether they are causing stress for the dolphin.

Fungie used to spend time with swimmers, but when boats arrived he would follow them and leave the swimmers. Then he used to spend time with small motor-boats, but now he doesn't – simply because there are so many of them. Neither does he chase all the speedboats that enter his area. Fungie was reported in 1989 to have been wounded by jet-skis, which many people are hoping to see banned from the harbour. Jet-skis can change direction much faster than boats, and they are a danger not only to the dolphin but to swimmers bobbing about in the water.

The congestion in the harbour causes problems for the fishermen also. The sheer number of boats and other craft at the harbour's mouth can make it difficult for the trawlers to enter or leave port. Large fishing boats cannot manoeuvre quickly and, with their bows rising high out of the water, the skippers at the wheelhouse can also find it difficult to see small objects ahead. Divers and swimmers bobbing to the surface can be in particular danger as a result. The smaller, inshore fishermen have had their work disturbed, too, by dinghies tying up to the buoys which mark their lobster pots' locations, and then, of course, dragging the marker and pots out of position.

Nobody could have foreseen years ago that one wild dolphin would attract tens of thousands of people to this beautiful, peaceful place. If they could have there might now be laws and rules to protect both man and animal. As it is there are no laws on this matter, except that dolphins are a protected species under the Irish Wildlife Act of 1976, which means that anyone who harms a dolphin can be prosecuted.

In the absence of laws and rules, it is important to use plenty of common sense. Fungie needs space. Anyone coming to see him should leave expensive machines like jet-skis and speedboats behind and instead take one of the dolphin boats that go out from the pier. Others may want to walk out to *Sláidín*, and here they can stand on the rocks and look out to the harbour's mouth. Swimmers who go into the water here may even find that Fungie will come to join them in their swim. They should stay quite close to the shore, because the tidal current at the harbour's mouth can flow at up to six knots, which is fast enough for even the strongest swimmer to get into difficulties.

Since Fungie's fame has spread, numbers of people have pitched their tents at *Sláidín*, but every person that camps there is bringing closer the day when the headland will disappear. Pressure on the rare community of plants here is killing off many of them. Where the sand has become exposed in the last few years, the storms of winter will work away, whipping the sand out and wearing down the headland.

Everyone who goes to see Fungie should respect him first of all and should respect, also, everyone else who happens to be visiting him at the same time. He gives his attention to all the boats, so there is no point in following him around. If you do, you may only make him feel hunted and bothered. If you bring a boat you should not try to lure him into a chase or constantly try to get close to him. Stop, wait, be patient. He'll come to you if he wants to. Unfortunately, there are a few people who seem to think that Fungie is some kind of plaything put there for their amusement, rather than a wild and independent creature. On the other side of the world volunteer rangers look after the well-being of Australia's special Bottlenose dolphins at Monkey Mia. It might be a good idea if a ranger could be appointed to look after our own special Bottlenose dolphin in Dingle.

Fungie could leave at any time. He is a wild dolphin and nothing is stopping him from heading out into the open sea and never coming back. One day, the boats that go out to see him at the harbour's mouth may not be able to find him, and gradually it will dawn on everyone that he has gone. Of course, having stayed so long, he could decide to stay until he dies. If so, his body will probably be found washed up on one of the shores that have been the boundaries of his home. But even when he has gone he will not be forgotten, because he has made an everlasting impression on the town of Dingle.

It would be hard to drive through Dingle today and not be aware of the significance of the dolphin to the town. At both the new and the old piers children queue with their parents for trips out to see Fungie. There are statues of him in shop windows and paintings of him on pub signs, and one pub is decorated with stained-glass dolphins. For sale are Fungie T-shirts, badges, stickers, posters, pendants, hats and postcards.

From the window of his house on a hill overlooking the town and harbour, retired fisherman Martin Flannery has a fine view of Fungie's home at the harbour's mouth. He can see him from as close as two feet when he regularly goes out on one of the boats for a visit. "He's like a pet dog to me. When I wasn't well for a few weeks I was mad to go out and see my old friend."

He never tires of knocking on the side of the boat with a brush-handle and watching the white tip of a snout swim up underneath it. He enjoys witnessing other people's excitement at seeing a dolphin for the first time. "Each time I am out with them I get excited too as if it's my own first time. You never get tired of seeing Fungie."

Tom Flannery, a distant relation of Martin's, also has a great affection for the dolphin. When not able to go out in a boat he'll walk down to *Sláidín* for a view of Fungie. Quiet-spoken, Tom has seen many of the dolphin's tricks. One scene he remembers particularly took place during

Martin Flannery

the summer of 1987. "A shellduck was standing over at Gravelly Point. She had about eight goslings with her and wanted to take them into the water. You could see, though, she was nervous about going in with the boats around. She waited for them all to be at a safe distance, then put out. But she hadn't seen Fungie waiting on her. He waited until she was a good bit out on the water and then up he went, jumping. He never stopped jumping around the poor duck and her young all the way up the south shore. But she made it."

Tom Hand recalls an incident when Fungie helped with a push in a breakdown. "There was a young lad in a small punt out in the harbour. His outboard engine cut out and wouldn't restart so he tried to row for shore. He was cutting across the tide so it wasn't easy. Fungie was up with us but then set off towards the boat. The next thing we saw he was up at the boat's stern pushing against it with his nose. He pushed him for a hundred yards across the tide. The lad in the boat never once realized why the rowing had become easier!"

John Griffin, owner of a garage in Dingle, has often had to contend with the dolphin trying to head him off when he has been coming up the harbour in his inflatable. "He would come at terrific speed and then take a short leap just in front. I would be drenched and have to slow down. Of course, that was what he wanted. He would take a quick pop up out of the water seconds later to investigate. When I could escape him and get out beyond his turning point he would make huge leaps out of the water. I don't know whether this was to attract me back or just his way of saying goodbye."

In Flahive's pub a clock marks the silence with its loud ticking. There are large pictures of Fungie on the walls. Peggy Flahive talks enthusiastically about dolphins and porpoises. "They're a wonderful creature. I was out there the other day, not a Christian near me, and he was going mad in the water, leaping and jumping." She remembers porpoises (or *tóithíns*) coming up the

harbour 20 years ago. "A pack of *tóithíns* chased sturgeon up around the harbour," she recalls.

"It was a great spectacle. Everybody stopped to watch them. We were hoping they would leave a sturgeon with us!"

From Flahive's pub there is a grandstand view of the pier from which literally thousands of children of all ages have left to go out in boats to see Fungie and have returned with bright eyes and glowing faces, and with memories of their meeting with a wild dolphin. Out there at the harbour's mouth boatloads of children often give him a noisier welcome than they'd give to a pop star stepping out of a limousine. The scenes are sometimes hilarious, with children darting to and fro as he moves from one side of the boat to the other. They hang over the sides, held firmly by parents, and dip their hands in the water only inches above the white-tipped snout of their new-found friend.

Two young people who met him while they were swimming are Daniel and Robert Hanrahan from Dalkey, then aged nine and twelve. "When I looked under me, Fungie was looking up at me," says Daniel. "He looked at me for ages. I was scared and thrilled at the same time."

Robert takes up the story. "When we were going back up the harbour I took a tow on the lifebelt. Fungie was moving with me all the time. Then he would come up and nudge me on my legs with his mouth."

Fungie followed Robert right into the upper reaches of the harbour – something he rarely does. Then, with the customary swing around, he was gone.

Fungie has filled many lives with magic and excitement. Long after he has gone he will come alive again in the light of a child's eyes as his story is told. A free spirit of the seas, he has given a special joy to those who have met him.

WHALE AND DOLPHIN ORGANIZATIONS

If you want to learn more about whales and dolphins and what is happening to them in the world, the organizations listed below will give you information. Membership is available in most cases.

WHALE AND DOLPHIN
CONSERVATION SOCIETY
20 West Lea Road
Bath
Avon BA1 3RL
England

INTERNATIONAL DOLPHIN
WATCH
Dolphin
Parklands
N. Ferriby
Humberside HU14 3ET
England

CETACEAN SOCIETY
INTERNATIONAL
190 Stillwold Drive
Wethersfield
Connecticut 06109
USA

GREENPEACE
44 Upper Mount Street
Dublin 2

INTERNATIONAL WHALING
COMMISSION
The Red House
Station Road
Histon
Cambridge CB4 4NP
England

CENTRE FOR STUDIES OF
WHALES AND DOLPHINS
Kopanjargatan 4d
Goteburg 213 C2
Sweden

DOLPHIN CIRCLE
38 Aldridge Road Villas
London W11
England

THE AMERICAN CETACEAN
SOCIETY
PO Box 2639
San Pedro CA 90731
USA

ORRCA
PO Box E293
St James
NSW2000
Australia

RECOMMENDED READING

DINGLE, Jack McKenna. Killarney Printing Works

THE DINGLE DOLPHIN, Ronnie Fitzgibbon. Irish Dolphin Research Society.

DOLPHINS, Jacques Yves Cousteau and Philippe Diole. Cassel.

DOLPHINS AND PORPOISES, Louise Quayle. Headline.

ENCOUNTERS WITH WHALES AND DOLPHINS, Wade Doak. Hodder and Stoughton.

FALLING FOR A DOLPHIN, Heathcote Williams. Jonathan Cape.

THE GREENPEACE BOOK OF DOLPHINS, John May (ed). Century Editions.

IRISH WHALES AND WHALING, James Fairley. Blackstaff Press.

THE MAGIC OF DOLPHINS, Horace Dobbs. Lutterworth Press.

THE NATURAL HISTORY OF WHALES AND DOLPHINS, Peter Evans. Christopher Helm.

WHALES, DOLPHINS AND PORPOISES, Sir Richard Harrison (ed). Merehurst Press.

WHALES OF THE WORLD, Nigel Bonner. Blandford.

WHALES OF THE WORLD, Lyall Watson. Hutchinson.

ACKNOWLEDGEMENTS

My appreciation to the following for their help: Dr Margaret Klinowska, scientific consultant and member of the Research Group in Mammalian Ecology and Reproduction, University of Cambridge, England, who acted as consultant editor on the chapter "A Dolphin's Life". Colm O'Riordan, marine biologist and former keeper of the Natural History Museum, for his comments and encouragement, and the International Whale and Dolphin Conservation Society which provided source material for the chapter "Threat to Dolphins". Kevin Flannery, marine officer for the Clare/Kerry region, and Declan Quigley, shared their extensive knowledge of marine life in Dingle; Kevin also gave me the photograph used on p.106. My thanks to Muriel for her comments on the manuscript, and to Joe, Michael and friends in LSL Photolab. I owe a great deal to Joe and Brid, Tommy, John and Dolores, Mark, Pat, Muiris and Noreen in the Star Bar; and to Martin and Mary, Paddy, Dave and Carmel, Jimmy and Jimmy, Peggy, Tomas, John and Maureen, Richie and Una for providing everything from food and lodgings and free boat trips to drying my clothes after being doused by a jumping dolphin. And, finally, my thanks to the fishermen of Dingle for drawing my attention to discoveries at sea and for their patience with all the boats now using the harbour.

This book is dedicated to my parents, Thomas and Elizabeth Mannion; to Noel and Catherine, my brother and sister; and to Monty.